The Martyrdom of Daniel and the Three Youths

TOOLS AND TRANSLATIONS

The Westar Tools and Translations series provides critical tools and fresh new translations for research on canonical and non-canonical texts that survive from the earliest periods of the Christian tradition to the Middle Ages. These writings are crucial for determining the complex history of Christian origins. The translations are known as the Scholars Version. Each work, whether a translation or research aid, is accompanied by textual notes, translation notes, cross references, and an index. An extensive introduction also sets out the challenge a text or research aid addresses.

EARLY CHRISTIAN APOCRYPHA

Editorial Board:
TONY BURKE
BRANDON HAWK
JANET SPITTLER

Translations of non-canonical texts out of the Christian tradition are offered as part of the Westar Tools and Translations series in cooperation with the North American Society for the Study of Christian Apocryphal Literature (NASSCAL). The Early Christian Apocrypha series features fresh new translations of major apocryphal texts that survive from the early period of the Christian church. These non-canonical writings are crucial for determining the complex history of Christian origins. The series continues the work of Julian V. Hills, who edited the first six volumes of the series for Polebridge Press. *Studies in Christian Apocrypha* is a subseries to *Early Christian Apocrypha*. The subseries features studies (including short introductions, monographs, and thematic collections of essays) on Christian Apocrypha from any time period and in any of its myriad forms—from early "lost gospel" papyri, through medieval hagiography and sermons incorporating apocryphal traditions, up to modern apocryphal "forgeries."

Volume 1: *The Acts of Andrew*
Volume 2: *The Epistle of the Apostles*
Volume 3: *The Acts of Thomas*
Volume 4: *The Acts of Peter*
Volume 5: *Didache*
Volume 6: *The Acts of John*
Volume 7: *The Protevangelium of James*
Volume 8: *The Gospel of Pseudo-Matthew and the Nativity of the Virgin*
Volume 9: *The Apocryphal Gospels: Jesus Traditions Outside the Bible*
Volume 10: *The Doctrine of Addai and the Letters of Jesus and Abgar*
Volume 11: *The Life of Thecla*
Volume 12: *The Martyrdom of Daniel and the Three Youths*

The Martyrdom of Daniel and the Three Youths

Alexey B. Somov

CASCADE *Books* • Eugene, Oregon

THE MARTYRDOM OF DANIEL AND THE THREE YOUTHS

Westar Tools and Translations
Early Christian Apocrypha 12

Copyright © 2025 Alexey B. Somov. All rights reserved. Except for brief quotations in critical publications or reviews, no part of this book may be reproduced in any manner without prior written permission from the publisher. Write: Permissions, Wipf and Stock Publishers, 199 W. 8th Ave., Suite 3, Eugene, OR 97401.

Cascade Books
An Imprint of Wipf and Stock Publishers
199 W. 8th Ave., Suite 3
Eugene, OR 97401

www.wipfandstock.com

PAPERBACK ISBN: 979-8-3852-4779-0
HARDCOVER ISBN: 979-8-3852-4780-6
EBOOK ISBN: 979-8-3852-4781-3

Cataloguing-in-Publication data:

Names: Somov, Alexey B., author.

Title: The martyrdom of Daniel and the three youths / Alexey B. Somov.

Description: Eugene, OR: Cascade Books, 2025. | Westar Tools and Translations: Early Christian Apocrypha 12. | Includes bibliographical references and index.

Identifiers: ISBN 979-8-3852-4779-0 (paperback). | ISBN 979-8-3852-4780-6 (hardcover). | ISBN 979-8-3852-4781-3 (ebook).

Subjects: LCSH: Early Christian Apocrypha—Criticism, interpretation, etc.

Classification: BS2840 S66 2025 (print). | BS2840 (ebook).

VERSION NUMBER 09/30/25

To my family

Contents

Preface | ix
Abbreviations | xii

Introduction | 1

1. The Heroic Deeds and the Contest of the Three Holy Youths and the Prophet Daniel | 39
2. The Sermon on the Demise of the Three Holy Youths and the All-Wise Daniel | 56

Appendix A: The Synaxarion and Chronicle Types of the Legend | 69

Appendix B: Further Development of the Legend in the Church Slavonic Tradition | 75

Bibliography | 89
Index of Ancient Sources | 97

Preface

IN THE 2011 ISRAELI movie *Footnote*, one of the main characters spent about thirty years reconstructing an unknown version of the Jerusalem Talmud basing his idea on a thorough analysis of numerous quotations in Jewish medieval writings. However, shortly before the publication of the first volume of his work, his colleague accidentally discovered an original copy of this version of the Talmud in a monastery in Italy. This made all the previous reconstruction work in vain. The idea that this version of the Talmud existed was confirmed, but no further reconstruction work was necessary. Sometimes these things happen to ancient documents. Having discovered the group of texts I was working on while writing this book, I often thought back to this movie. On the one hand, this is not what I would wish for any scholar who has worked hard to reconstruct ancient texts or ideas, but on the other, such discoveries greatly improve our knowledge and move us far ahead in our research. This is the story of the martyrdom of Daniel and the Three Youths. Already some early Christian authors regarded these biblical righteous ones not only as an example of miraculous deliverance from imminent death, but also as martyrs or as a pattern of Christian martyrdom. However, they do not provide us with any proof of their real martyrdom. But the legend with which the present book deals goes much further and presents an account of the real martyrdom of Daniel and his three companions, despite other traditions on their peaceful departure. The further details of this fascinating and not well-known story, which is a motley fabric of biblical, parabiblical traditions, folkloric elements, and unexpected exegetical solutions that transfer the biblical heroes of the Hebrew Bible/Old Testament into the world of Early Christianity/New Testament, follow below.

Preface

I happened to come across a mention of this legend in 2019 while reading an article on the Three Youths in the *Orthodox Encyclopedia*.[1] Then, it became one of my main topics during my research fellowship at the Centre for Advanced Studies "Beyond Canon: Heterotopias of Religious Authority in Late Antique Christianity" (FOR 2770/1) at Universität Regensburg (January 2019 to July 2020). As a result of this fellowship, I have published a research article that investigates the origins and development of the Martyrdom of Daniel and the Three Youths in the Greek, Church Slavonic, and Armenian versions. To this work I occasionally refer in the present book.[2] However, the framework of the article did not allow me to provide a general introduction to this legend and, just as importantly, has prevented me from introducing readers to the full text of this martyrdom. This is what has been done in this book, which is the fruit of my second research fellowship at "Beyond Canon" (February 2023 to February 2025). Without the generous support of this Centre and the resources and facilities of Universität Regensburg, this work could not have been accomplished and I am sincerely thankful for this.

I would like to express my personal gratitude to the director general of "Beyond Canon," Prof. Dr. Tobias Nicklas, and the co-director, Prof. Dr. Harald Buchinger, for their support and the important suggestions they made regarding my research. I also sincerely thank the Centre team, Dr. Stephany Hallinger, Charlotte von Schelling, Franziska J. A. Müller, Dr. Alesja Lavrinoviča, as well as my colleagues and friends from "Beyond Canon," especially Dr. Arkadiy Avdokhin for his very important suggestions on the difficulties of the Greek text of the legend, Prof. Dr. Jan Bremmer, Dr. Dariya Syroyid, and Dr. Emmanuela Valeriani for their suggestions and comments. My special thanks go to Dr. David Clark for his careful reading and correction of the manuscript.

Further, I wish to thank the editors of the Early Christian Apocrypha Series, Dr. Tony Burke, Dr. Brandon Hawk, and Dr. Janet Spittler, for accepting my work for the series and for the careful reading, corrections, and suggestions they made to my manuscript. Special thanks to Slavomír Čéplö for his review of my translations of the Church Slavonic texts, and to the editorial staff at Wipf and Stock, especially Matthew Wimer, K. C. Hanson,

---

1. Nikitin, Tkachenko, and Lukashevich, "Children in Babylon." Unfortunately, this article only briefly mentions this martyrdom.
2. Somov, "Martyrdom of Daniel."

Preface

and ace copy editor Elisabeth Rickard, for guiding the book through publication.

In addition, I would like to express my gratitude to my friends and colleagues Dr. Ivan Miroshnikov and Jan Shavrin for their feedback and assistance at several stages of my working on this book, and, of course, to my family, especially my wife Anna Somova for her patience, warm encouragement, and tireless help.

Alexey B. Somov
Regensburg, Germany
May 2024

Abbreviations

Ancient

Acta Fruct.	*Acta SS. Fructuosi, Augurii et Eulogii*
Acts Andr. Phlm.	*Acts of Andrew and Philemon*
Apoc. Pet.	*Apocalypse of Peter*
Apos. Con.	*Apostolic Constitutions*

Augustine
    Adv. Jud.   *Tractatus adv. Judaeos*
    Serm.   *Sermons*

4 Bar.   4 Baruch (Paraleipomena Jeremiou)

Bardaisan of Edessa
    Bk. Laws   *Book of the Laws of the Countries*

Barn.   *Barnabas*

Basil the Great
    Ep.   *Epistolae*

b. Sanh.   Babylonian Talmud, *Sanhedrin*

Clement of Alexandria
    Paed.   *Paedagogus*
    Strom.   *Stromateis*

Abbreviations

Constantinus Manasses
- *Syn. Hist.* — *Synopsis Chronike*

Cyprian
- *Ep.* — *Epistles*
- *Fort.* — *Ad fortunatum*
- *Laps.* — *De lapsis*

1 En.   1 Enoch (Ethiopic Apocalypse)
2 En.   2 Enoch (Slavonic Apocalypse)

Ephrem the Syrian
- *Hymn Fast.* — *Hymns on the Fast*
- *Hymn Nat.* — *Hymns on the Nativity*

Epiphanius of Salamis
- *Ancor.* — *Ancoratus*
- *Pan.* — *Panarion*

Ep Jer   Epistle of Jeremiah

Eusebius of Caesarea
- *Dem. ev.* — *Demenstratio evangelica*
- *Ecl. proph.* — *Eclogae propheticae*
- *Praep. ev.* — *Praeparatio evangelica*

Gen. Rab.   *Genesis Rabbah*
Gk. Apoc. Ezra   *Greek Apocalypse of Ezra*
Gos. Nic.   *Gospel of Nicodemus*

Gregory of Nazianzus
- *Hom.* — *Homilies*

Gregory of Nyssa
- *Diem nat.* — *In diem natalem*

Abbreviations

Herodotus
    Hist.   *Histories*

Hippolytus
    Comm. Dan. *Commentarium in Danielum*

Ignatius
    Magn.   *To the Magnesians*

Irenaeus of Lyons
    Epid.   *Epideixis tou apostolikou kērygmatos*
    Haer.   *Adversus haereses*

Isidor of Pelusium
    2.177 *Theod.* Book 2 Letter 177 to
         Presb. Presbyter Theodotus

Jer. Apocr.   *Jeremiah Apocryphon*

John Chrysostom
    Adv. Jud.   *Adversus Judaeos*

Justin
    Dial.   *Dialogus cum Tryphone*

Lactantius
    Inst.   *Divinarum institutionum*

LAE   Life of Adam and Eve
Liv. Pro.   Lives of the Prophets
Mart. Dan.   *Martyrdom of Daniel and the Three Youths*
Mart. Jul. Basil. *Martyrdom of Julian and Basilissa*
Mart. Perp. Felic. *Martyrdom of Perpetua and Felicity*
Mart. Pol.   *Martyrdom of Polycarp*
Mart. Tar. Prob. *Martyrdom of Tarachus, Probus*
        Andr.   *and Andronicus*
Mart. Theod.   *Martyrdom of Theodotus*

Abbreviations

Men. Basil II   Menologion of Basil II

Origen

    Comm. Cant.   Commentarius in Canticum

    Comm. Rom.   Commentarii in Romanos

Pan. 3 Child.   Panegyric of the Three Children of Babylon

Pirqe R. El.   Pirqe Rabbi Eliezer

Polychronius of Apamea

    Comm. Dan.   Commentarii in Danielem

Pseudo-Clement

    Rec.   Recognitions

Pseudo-Cyprian

    De laude mart.   De laude martyrii

    De pasch.   De pascha computes

Sg Three   Song of the Three Young Men

Sermo de obit.   Sermo de obitu sanctorum trium puerorum

Shir Rab.   Shir Ha-Shirim Rabbah

T. Levi   Testament of Levi

T. Mos.   Testament of Moses

Tertullian

    An.   De anima

    Marc.   Adversus Marcionem

    Prax.   Adversus Praxean

    Res.   De resurrectione carnis

Theodoret of Cyrus

    Interp. Dan.   Interpretatio in Danielem

Vis. Ezra   Vision of Ezra

Vit. Mac. Rom.   Vita sancti Macarii Romani

ABBREVIATIONS

Modern

AB	Anchor Bible
AnBoll	*Analecta Bollandiana*
BHG	*Bibliotheca Hagiographica Graeca*. Edited by François Halkin. 3 vols. 3rd ed. Brussels: Société des bollandistes, 1986
CAVT	*Clavis Apocryphum Veteris Testamenti*. Edited by Jean-Claude Haelewyck. Turnhout: Brepols, 1998
CEJL	Commentaries on Early Jewish Literature
CurBR	*Currents in Biblical Research*
EJL	Early Judaism and Its Literature
FOTL	Forms of the Old Testament Literature
GCS	Die griechischen christlichen Schriftsteller der ersten [drei] Jahrhunderte
HTR	*Harvard Theological Review*
JBL	*Journal of Biblical Literature*
JSP	*Journal for the Study of the Pseudepigrapha*
LNTS	The Library of New Testament Studies
Mus	*Muséon: Revue d'études orientales*
NovT	*Novum Testamentum*
NPNF²	*Nicene and Post-Nicene Fathers*, Series 2
NTOA	Novum Testamentum et Orbis Antiquus
OE	*The Orthodox Encyclopedia*. Moscow: The Orthodox Encyclopedia, 2000– (in Russian)
Or	*Orientalia* (NS)
OrChrAn	Orientalia Christiana Analecta
PG	*Patrologia Graeca*. Edited by Jacques-Paul Migne. 162 vols. Paris, 1857–86
PO	*Patrologia Orientalis*
RAC	*Reallexikon für Antike und Christentum*. Edited by Theodor Klauser et al. Stuttgart: Hiersemann, 1950–
RevScRel	*Revue des sciences religieuses*
RGRW	Religions in the Graeco-Roman World

Abbreviations

SGLG	Sammlung griechischer und lateinischer Grammatiker
StPB	Studia Post-biblica
SUNT	Studien zur Umwelt des Neuen Testaments
SVTP	Studia in Veteris Testamenti Pseudepigraphica
Syn. Alex.	Basset, René. "Le Synaxaire arabe jacobite (rédaction copte)." *PO* 16 (1922) 186–424
VC	*Vigiliae Christianae*
WBC	Word Biblical Commentary
WGRW	Writings from the Greco-Roman World
WUNT	Wissenschaftliche Untersuchungen zum Neuen Testament

Conventions

LXX	Septuagint
MT	Masoretic text
OG	Old Greek translation of the Old Testament
Th.	Theodotion's translation of the Old Testament

Sigla

Mart. Dan.

V	Vatican, Biblioteca Apostolica Vaticana, Barb. gr. 481 (13th cent.)
P	Paris, Bibliothèque nationale de France, Gr. 1491 (9th/10th cent.)
B	Oxford, Bodleian Library, Laud. gr. 69 (11th cent.)
C	Paris, Bibliothèque nationale de France, Coislin 105 (10th/11th cent.)
M	Partial edition from unidentified source in Migne, *PG* 77:1117–18
Men.	*Great Menaion Reader*
SlavR	Moscow, Russian State Library, F. 178 #3127 (16th cent.)

Abbreviations

SlavM   Moscow, Moscow Theological Academy, F. 173/I #90 (16th cent.)

SlavU   Moscow, Russian State Library, V.M. Undolsky 560 (15th/16th cent.)

Sermo de obit.

R   Rome, Biblioteca Vallicelliana, F 33 (16th cent.)

D   Paris, Bibliothèque nationale de France, Coislin 121 (14th cent.)

SlavZ   Lviv, Scientific Library of Ivan Franko National University, #203.III 16th cent.)

UkS   Transcarpathia, Shevchenko Institute of Literature of the National Academy of Science of Ukraine, f.3 #769 (17th/18th cent.)

Additional sources

Alexandria[2]   *Alexandria*, 2nd ed. (mid-15th cent.)

Alexandria[4]   *Alexandria*, 4th ed. (16th cent.)

Arm.   Yerevan, Matenadaran, 1500 (13th cent.)

Arm. Syn.[2]   Armenian Synaxarion, 2nd ed. (1269)

Arm. Syn.[4]   Armenian Synaxarion, 4th ed. (15th cent.)

Syn. Cp.   Synaxarion of Constantinople

Men. Basil II   Menologion of Basil II

Introduction

THE FIGURE OF THE prophet Daniel and basic details of his legendary life are known from the biblical book that bears his name. These details include such features as his incredible faithfulness to God and his commandments, his abilities to interpret dreams and mysteries, his apocalyptic visions, his interpretation of the destruction of the golden statue, and his rescue from the lions' den. The Three Youths—Hananias, Azarias, and Misael (Hebrew: Hananiah, Azariah, and Mishael)—are also heroes of the book of Daniel. Together with Daniel they are placed among the captive Israelites and taken to the palace of the Babylonian king (Dan 1). They are the main characters of Dan 3, which tells of their miraculous delivery from death in the fiery furnace and subsequent exaltation by King Nebuchadnezzar. Daniel, too, endures a near-martyrdom when he is consigned to the lions' den (Dan 6). The author does not reveal much about what happened to the Three Youths apart from their appointment "over the affairs of the province of Babylon" (Dan 2:49 and 3:30); as for Daniel, his fate is directly mentioned in the final verses of the book: "But you, go your way, and rest; you shall rise for your reward at the end of the days" (Dan 12:13). This can be interpreted as a reference to his peaceful death and his resurrection at the end of time. Most of the later traditions about Daniel, indeed, indicate his departure in peace (e.g., "And the holy man fell asleep in peace"; Liv. Pro. 4:21). Nevertheless, some early Christian writings hint at the actual martyrdom of Daniel and his three companions.[1] Already Hippolytus of Rome (170–235 CE) likens the episode of the Three Youths in the fiery furnace to martyrdom (*Comm. Dan.* 2.30.1) and links Daniel and his three companions to the Maccabean martyrs (2.35.8–9), who became a pattern for Christian martyrdom.[2] The

---

1. Somov, "Martyrdom of Daniel," 209–11.
2. Tucker, "Early Wirkungsgeschichte," 298.

The Martyrdom of Daniel and the Three Youths

Maccabees are also associated with Daniel and the Three Youths by Gregory of Nazianzus (*Hom.* 5.40) as well as in some passages from Cyprian and Origen.[3] In addition, the story of the Three Youths is called a martyrdom in Cyprian (*Laps.* 31; cf. *Fort.* 11) and Pseudo-John Chrysostom (*De tribus pueris et de fornace Babylonica*; PG 56:593–600), or is equated with martyrdom in some other Christian writings.[4]

Connections between the Three Youths and the Maccabean martyrs go back to the origins of the book of Daniel. It is a composite work that consists of two parts: the narrative "court tales" about the life of Daniel and his three companions (chaps. 1–6) and Daniel's apocalyptic visions (chaps. 7–12). It is suggested that the book was written and edited in several stages. Chaps. 2–6 may have been composed in the Persian period. As the Three Youths do not appear after chapter 3, they might have originally functioned as independent figures and were not associated with Daniel.[5] Chap. 1 serves as an introduction to the tales and was added during the Hellenistic period. Chap. 7 looks to have been written during the persecution of Antiochus IV Epiphanes, but before the desecration of the temple. Chaps. 8–12 could have been added between 167 and 164 BCE, and 12:11–12 inserted before the rededication of the temple.[6] Moreover, Dan 2–6 may have been reedited in Maccabean times to bring it into unity with Dan 7–12.[7] At this time, the editors "placed a hagiographical frame around the old stories of faithfulness in the face of death" in order to conform with the later chapters of Daniel and to make Daniel and the Three Youths the precursors and proto-martyrs of those "wise" leaders who suffered from the wicked king in Dan 11:35–38 and then were promised to be resurrected in Dan 12:2–3.[8] Therefore, Dan 3 and 6 could be reinterpreted as metaphors for the martyrdom and resurrection of the oppressed righteous ones of Maccabean times.[9] In addition, it is not to be excluded that the promise of resurrection to the Maccabean martyrs in 2 Macc 7 and the

---

3. See Vinson, "Gregory Nazianzen's Homily 15," 173–75.

4. More references to the Three Youths as martyrs from rabbinic and patristic sources can be found in Brakmann et al., "Jünglinge im Feuerofen," 356–57, 360–61; and Tucker, "Early Wirkungsgeschichte."

5. Collins, *Commentary*, 179.

6. See Collins, *Commentary*, 27–38, for more detail about the origins of several parts of Daniel.

7. Collins, "Court-Tales," 218.

8. Grillo, *Daniel After Babylon*, 34.

9. Collins, *Commentary*, 60–61, 194.

Introduction

eschatological resurrection in Dan 12:2–3 are connected.[10] Moreover, Th. Dan 3:51–90 (the *Song of the Three Youths*), which is a further development of the book of Daniel,[11] may have been interpreted as relating to both the death and subsequent resurrection of the righteous:

> Bless the Lord, Hananias, Azarias, Misael; sing hymns to him and highly exalt him forever. For he has rescued us from Hades and saved us from the power of death, and delivered us from the midst of the burning flame of the furnace and delivered us from the middle of the fire. (*Sg Three* 66; =Th. Dan 3:88; trans. NETS)

In Eastern Orthodox tradition, Th. Dan 3:1–88 is included in the liturgical readings on the Great Saturday liturgy as one of the prophecies about the resurrection of Jesus. The use of this passage in the liturgical practice of Easter services has been known since the fourth or even the third century CE.[12]

The next basis for the connection between Daniel, the Three Youths, and the Maccabean martyrs is found in 4 Maccabees. In this text, which further develops the story about the Maccabean martyrs from 2 Macc 6–7, Daniel and his three companions are directly compared with the martyrs:

> The lions surrounding Daniel were not so savage, nor was the furnace of Misael so ablaze with fiercest fire as the nature of her maternal love inflamed her when she saw her seven sons tortured in such diverse ways. (4 Macc 16:3; trans. NETS)

> Daniel the righteous was thrown to the lions, and Hananias, Azarias and Misael were hurled into a furnace of fire and, for the sake of God, endured. (4 Macc 16:21 ; trans. NETS)

Thus, although Daniel and the Three Youths are delivered from physical death after their persecution (Dan 3 and 6), they are, nevertheless, sometimes compared or even equated with the Maccabean martyrs who died for their faithfulness to the Jewish Law in 2 Macc 7 and 4 Maccabees.[13]

---

10. Goldstein, *II Maccabees*, 306; Wright, *Resurrection of the Son of God*, 150–53, 202; and Kellermann, "Danielbuch," 51–70.

11. Collins, *Commentary*, 38.

12. Dulaey, "Trois Hébreux," 46; and Seeliger, "Παλαι Μαρτυρες," 302–6.

13. There may have been a distinction, however, between a martyr as a person who witnesses and dies and a confessor who witnesses but is delivered from torture; see Grillo, *Daniel After Babylon*, 32. Cf. Augustine, *Serm.* 286: "If they had died in the fire, they would have received the crown of martyrdom in secret, and it would have been no good to this king. That's why they were preserved for a time, so that the unbeliever might come to believe, the one who had condemned them might come to praise God. The God

The martyred Maccabees were probably regarded as imitating the resistance to persecution displayed by Daniel and the Three Youths.[14] The three righteous ones were regarded also as a pattern of faith (1 Macc 2:59; Heb 11:34; Cyprian, *Ep.* 58.5), which in early Christian discourse is identified with faith in eternal life and salvation (e.g., Cyprian, *Ep.* 6.3; Ps.-Cyprian, *De laude mart.* 12).[15] The point of contact between 2 Macc 7, 4 Maccabees, and Dan 3 is found not only in the fact of the persecution of the righteous at the hand of a wicked pagan king, but also in the promise of their future resurrection. Indeed, Hippolytus of Rome states that the Three Youths were saved from Hades (*Comm. Dan.* 2.29.12), while Ps.-Cyprian identifies the fire in the furnace with the flames of Gehenna (*De pasch.* 17; *De laude mart.* 12). Both writers could have deduced this idea from 2 Maccabees (7:9, 14, 23).

Furthermore, Dan 3 was used as an argument for the resurrection of the body (Irenaeus, *Haer.* 5.5.2; Tertullian, *Res.* 58.6–10). Hippolytus uses the example of the Three Youths' faithfulness to the Lord in the fiery furnace, which he considers a kind of martyrdom, as a reference to resurrection of the flesh (σαρκὸς ἀνάστασιν). For him, the fact that their clothes were not damaged in the fire indicates that our perishable nature will be resurrected, because it is in contact with our immortal (holy) soul (*Comm. Dan.* 2.28.3–5).[16]

Apart from all these implicit references to the martyrdom of the Three Youths, there is a group of Christian texts that goes much further and is directly devoted to telling the story of their actual martyrdom. This group can be called "Legends of the Martyrdom of Daniel and the Three Youths" (hereafter *Legend*). The texts share a unique and intriguing plot: they narrate not the peaceful departure of Daniel and his three companions but their martyrdom for Christ at the hand of a certain wicked Persian king and their subsequent resurrection. This resurrection is directly linked to the resurrection of Jesus and the story about the risen holy ones

---

of the three boys was the same as the God of the Maccabees. He delivered the first ones from the fire, he had the latter die in the fire. Did he chop and change? Did he love those more than these? A more splendid crown was given to the Maccabees" (trans. Hill).

14. Ziadé, *Martyrs Maccabées*, 87; and Joslyn-Siemiatkoski, *Christian Memories*, 21.

15. Dulaey, "Trois Hébreux," 34–36.

16. The link between the deliverance of the Three Youths from the furnace and eschatological resurrection was also established in rabbinic Jewish tradition (cf. *Pirqe R. El.* 33). See further examples from the rabbinic tradition in Dulaey, "Trois Hébreux," 47.

in Matt 27:52–53 and appears as an exegetical attempt to identify those who were resurrected.

To what category of the apocryphal traditions does this martyrdom belong? In fact, Daniel is a hero of multiple post-biblical legends and traditions. Lorenzo DiTommaso divides these legends into two categories: the Daniel apocrypha of the Second Temple period (e.g., the Greek additions to Daniel; the Qumran fragments of the *Prayer of Nabonidus* [4Q242], 4Q*Pseudo-Daniel* $^{a-b}$ [4Q243/244], and 4Q*Pseudo-Daniel*^{c} [4Q245], 4Q*Apocryphon of Daniel ar* [4Q246], Josephus' *Jewish Antiquities*, and Liv. Pro.) and the Daniel texts of the late antique and early medieval periods. The latter is represented by multiple texts surviving in several languages (Hebrew, Aramaic, Greek, Latin, Armenian, Syriac, Coptic, Arabic, Church Slavonic, and others), which include stories about Daniel's life, visions, apocalyptic oracles, astronomical and geomantic texts, and dream manuals as well as tales about the Three Youths, Susanna, and Nebuchadnezzar.[17] The *Legend* belongs to the second category and is an example of the Daniel legenda (see below) that retell and reflect the story of Daniel and his three companions in Dan 1–6.[18] It is interesting that although Daniel is mentioned in the title, as well as in the text of the *Legend* itself, his involvement in all the events is more indirect and tacit than that of the Three Youths who become the main characters of the story.

The *Legend* was adapted for liturgical, hagiographical, and even iconographical needs. It was transmitted in different forms that vary in their content and scope of events. For instance, sometimes it contains only the account of the martyrdom of Daniel and the Three Youths, while at other times it also includes the story about their lives and deeds in Babylon. The texts that contain the *Legend* can be divided into three types: the homiletical type, the synaxarion type, and the chronicle type. The homiletical type of the *Legend* is embedded in a lengthy narrative arranged in the form of a homily to be read during Christian worship. The synaxarion type is a text of the martyrdom found in the Synaxarion—a liturgical book containing the lives of the saints to be read on feast days arranged according to the church calendar. The chronological type is a very condensed recension of the martyrdom found in one of the Church Slavonic editions of the historical chronicle called *Alexandria*.

---

17. DiTommaso, *Book of Daniel*, 6–12.
18. DiTommaso, *Book of Daniel*, 13.

The *Legend* is occasionally mentioned by scholars who study the apocryphal Daniel literature, but apart from a few exceptions, without detailed analysis. As M. R. James puts it: "It is a curious tale, to which little attention has been paid."[19] The most representative and probably most ancient recensions of the *Legend* in Greek[20] and Church Slavonic[21] were published by V. M. Istrin. These two recensions are titled "The heroic deeds and the contest of the Three Holy Youths and the prophet Daniel" (*CAVT* 267; *BHG* 484z, 484*; hereafter *Mart. Dan.* from *Martyrium tribus pueris et Danielis Prophetae*) and "The Sermon on the Demise of the Three Holy Youths and the All-Wise Daniel by Our Holy Father Cyril, Archbishop of Alexandria" (*CAVT* 267; *BHG* 487, 487a; hereafter *Sermo de obit.* from *Sermo de obitu sanctorum trium puerorum*). These recensions are the main focus of this book, but other versions of the *Legend* will also be discussed.

Summary

Both recensions of the *Legend* published by Istrin are set in the form of a homily. They begin with a solemn introduction to the good way of life and death of Daniel and the Three Youths as a pattern for the life of the church. The men are described as Christian martyrs and confessors of the resurrection from the dead. In both recensions the author refers to a portion of Scripture that was read during the church service dedicated to these saints and commemorated on 17 December, according to the calendar of the Eastern Orthodox church. It is not clear what passage was read but probably it was Dan 3 (1:1–4).[22]

Section 1 covers the time spent by the characters in Babylon. It begins with a lament over Jerusalem based on four compound quotations and allusions from Isaiah, Amos, and Psalms, cited as four predictions against the sins of the inhabitants of Jerusalem and their subsequent punishment by God (1:5–9). The siege of the city by King Nebuchadnezzar and his troops is

---

19. James, *Lost Apocrypha*, 70. Brakmann et al., "Jünglinge im Feuerofen," 374; DiTommaso, *Book of Daniel*, 78–79, 508 (includes mention of one Church Slavonic version); and Stone, *Patriarchs and Prophets*, 134, 154–57; Stone, *Adam to Daniel*, 220–37 (Armenian versions).

20. Istrin, "Greek Copies," 1–18.

21. Istrin, *Alexandria*, appendix 345–56.

22. Citations are to both texts where their contents align; at other times separate citations are provided.

Introduction

the instrument of this punishment. Nebuchadnezzar comes to the walls of Jerusalem with a great and well-trained army at the third hour of the night (1:10–11). According to the story, there is a great feast in the city, a feast described as a pagan celebration with orgies, dancing, and drunkenness, in which all the inhabitants of the city participate without exception. Only the prophets Jeremiah, Baruch, and Abimelech are kept outside the city, lamenting over its destiny (1:11–13). This detail is taken from a parabiblical tradition of 4 Baruch and other legendary traditions about Jeremiah. The Babylonian attack starts with the great sound of trumpets, the roar of warhorses, and the clang of siege machines. The walls of Jerusalem fall, the city is captured, the temple is destroyed, and all the sacred vessels and other worship equipment are taken to Babylon (1:14–17).

Daniel and the Three Youths also journey to Babylon together with other Jewish captives numbering forty thousand in total. They are barefoot, bound together, dragged through uneven and impassable places, and beaten badly along the way (2:1–4). Upon their arrival in Babylon, which is situated on the third river (*Mart. Dan.* 2:5) or the river Stoigion (*Sermo de obit.* 2:5; see also Asidon in UkS), the captives are commanded to sing psalms as they did in their homeland and to play the lyres, which are hung on willows. However, the Three Youths refuse because for them, as Jews, it is impossible to speak the words of God before the ritually unclean gentiles (2:5–6). The Three Youths can praise the Lord only silently. For their refusal, the Youths are severely caned for several hours by the king's officials. About the third hour of night, God sends angels to heal them and turn the hearts of their enemies to be merciful toward them (2:7–8). Then Daniel and the Three Youths explain to Nebuchadnezzar the meaning of his dream (as in Dan 2). For this they are exalted by the king and appointed to be rulers of his whole kingdom (2:9).

Then, although three kingdoms change in Babylon, Nebuchadnezzar, strangely enough, continues to reign. During this time the Jews do not worship pagan gods and remain faithful to the Lord. Moreover, Daniel and the Three Youths smash the golden idol of sixty cubits (cf. Dan 3), destroy Bel, and kill the dragon of sixty cubits (cf. Bel 1:1–27) (3:1–3). Here *Mart. Dan.* reveals that these stories derive from "crystal plates" and until now were "completely unknown" (3:3; cf. the reference in *Sermo de obit.* 3:4 to "hidden books of Daniel"). The *Legend* then briefly narrates Daniel's imprisonment in the lions' den (Dan 6; Bel 1:28–42) followed by an extensive account of the Three Youths' deliverance from the fiery furnace

(Dan 3). After the Youths are thrown into the furnace, the archangel Michael cools them down with water or dew; they rejoice and glorify God right in the middle of the fire (3:4–5). The Lord's Spirit is likened to "a moist breeze whistling on them" (*Mart. Dan.* 3:5; cf. "the wind of dew was whistling" in *Sermo de obit.* 3:5). The Three Youths' hair, faces, clothes, and sandals remain unburned. Then King Nebuchadnezzar is astonished to see four people in the furnace instead of three (3:6). Azarias rebukes the king for his ignorance of God which makes it impossible for him to recognize the Son of God among them. He then declares that this Son of God, who will be born from the virgin and come in flesh, and for whom they suffered in the furnace, had appeared to them there and appointed them to be martyrs for his sake (3:7).

From here the story continues into Nebuchadnezzar's vision of the descent of the Holy One from Th. Dan 4:13–17, though the *Legend* blends the two stories together and does not turn the focus on Daniel. The king sees the Holy One, who could be an angel or the Son of God. Azarias declares that what Nebuchadnezzar saw was the Son of God who will come in flesh in the future. The king comes to his senses, wishes peace to his subjects, and appoints the Three Youths to administrative positions as rulers over Babylon. Four months later Nebuchadnezzar, who had turned to the God of Israel, departs peacefully (3:8–10).

Section 2 of the *Legend* focuses on the martyrdom and resurrection of Daniel and the Three Youths. Four months after Nebuchadnezzar's death, another king seizes power in Babylon: Atticus the Persian, son of Magedon, who rules his kingdom for thirty-four years (4:1). It is not possible to identify Atticus nor Magedon with any historical kings of that period. Atticus is described as a pagan king who enquires about the Babylonian decrees and investigates the details about the captive Jews in Babylon. He orders Daniel and the Three Youths to be arrested and interrogated. They are brought before the king for judgment and asked about their faith, their way of thinking, and their family. The Three Youths play a major role in the controversy with Atticus, bravely standing before the king to answer his questions (4:1–2). Misael, who is the youngest of the three brothers, is chosen as their speaker before the king; the others consider it an abomination to speak with a pagan. Instead of answering Atticus's questions, Misael starts by rebuking the king's paganism (4:3–7). Misael's rebuke is based on a mixture of several prejudices about Zoroastrians and, oddly enough, Manichaeans. Thus, Atticus's paganism includes worshiping fire,

Introduction

depicting his god as a dog or a wolf, burning cows' offspring as a sacrifice, and eating the mixture of its blood with dough, which, as Misael asserts, is why Atticus is a Manichaean.

After these accusations, Misael begins to answer the king's questions about the Three Youths' family (*Mart. Dan.* 4:8–9; *Sermo de obit.* 4:8–10). Their parents are Hezekiah and Kallegonia (Hezekiah's wife is named Hephzibah in 2 Kgs 21:1). This Hezekiah was a king of Judah, who was deadly sick but was healed after his pious prayer of repentance and was granted fifteen more years of his life by the Lord (cf. 2 Kgs 20:1–11). In Misael's words, it was Hezekiah who prophesied to the Three Youths about the incarnation of the Word of God, whom they saw while in the fiery furnace and for whom they were ready to receive death. In contrast to Nebuchadnezzar, who turned to the true God, Atticus is not deemed worthy of salvation (*Mart. Dan.* 4:9; *Sermo de obit.* 4:16–17). Angry at Misael's speech, Atticus orders him to be beheaded (5:1). When Misael's head is cut off, Azarias runs up, stretches his cloak, and receives the head into the cloak, weeping. The king then decides to behead Azarias also. The third Youth, Hannaias, receives Azarias's and Misael's severed heads into his cloak and holds them to his bosom before also losing his head, but not before saying that they would go together to the Lord Savior of the world. All three heads are received by Daniel into his robe and, as expected, he is decapitated along with them (5:1–3).

Their collective martyrdom happens on 17 December (*Sermo de obit.* 5:8; cf. the note to *Mart. Dan.* 5:3). All the Jews greatly mourn for them. On the third day after the martyrdom, the Jews collect some silver and enlist silversmiths to make coffins for the four men and engrave their names on each one. Their remains are placed within, and suddenly each of their heads rejoin their bodies (5:4). Since Atticus wanted to burn their bodies together with their coffins, angels come at night and carry them to Mount Gebal, hiding them there under a rock (5:5). The remains of Daniel and his three companions rest there for 440 years (*Mart. Dan.* 5:10; preserved partially in *Sermo de obit.* 4:10). Then, after the Jews return from Babylon to Judea and Jerusalem is restored, their bodies somehow return to Babylon and remain there until the birth of Jesus (*Mart. Dan.* 5:5).

The *Legend* then describes several cataclysmic events that occur during Jesus' crucifixion: the shaking of the foundations of the earth and heaven, the shattering of rocks into pieces, and the shaking of mountains. Then, the storehouses of Hades are enlightened and the bodies of certain saints are resurrected; they appear to many people in Jerusalem and even talk with them (*Mart. Dan.* 5:6; *Sermo de obit.* 4:11; cf. Matt 27:51–53). Among the saints are Abel, Noah, Abraham, Isaac, Jacob, Joseph, Isaiah, Jeremiah, Baruch, John the Baptist, Hezekiah, and Kallegonia, as well as Daniel and the Three Youths and other people—more than 500 in total (*Mart. Dan.* 5:7; *Sermo de obit.* 4:12). This number is taken from 1 Cor 15:6, which speaks of Jesus appearing to 500 disciples after his resurrection (*Mart. Dan.* 5:8 makes the connection of this event to Jesus' resurrection explicit). These 500 go immediately to paradise (preceded by the Good Thief of Luke 23:40–43 in *Sermo de obit.* 4:14); others go back to sleep until the second coming (*Mart. Dan.* 5:8–9; *Sermo de obit.* 4:13–15). As for the Three Youths and Daniel, they are brought back "to their own place" (*Mart. Dan.* 5:10).

The story of the martyrdom ends here in *Mart. Dan.* but continues in *Sermo de obit.* 5:5–7 with a closing statement about the glorification of Jesus Christ, further honoring of the martyrs, and a calling to the faithful to follow the martyrs' righteousness and virtue.

Textual History

The textual history of the *Legend* is organized according to three types: the homiletical type, the synaxarion type, and the chronicle type.

The Homiletical Type

The homiletical type of the *Legend* is a lengthy narrative arranged in the form of a homily to be read during a service of Christian worship. The Greek version of this type survives in two recensions: *Mart. Dan.* and *Sermo de obit.* Both recensions were published by V. M. Istrin in 1901.[23] Istrin's edition of *Mart. Dan.* is based on Vatican, Biblioteca Apostolica Vaticana, Barb. gr. 481, fols. 186v–191r (13th cent.; =V). Istrin also consulted three other manuscripts of earlier date:

> Paris, Bibliothèque nationale de France, gr. 1491, fols. 40r–44r (9th/10th cent.; =P) Oxford, Bodleian Library, Laud. gr. 69, fols. 235v–240v (11th cent.; =B) Paris, Bibliothèque nationale de France, Coislin 105, fols. 133r–135r, 140v–142r (10th/11th cent.; =C); this manuscript terminates at the end of ch. 3.

23. Istrin, "Greek Copies."

Introduction

Since the publication of Istrin's edition, more manuscripts containing *Mart. Dan.* have been discovered, but they have not yet been analyzed and published. There are now thirty-eight extant witnesses ranging from the ninth to the fifteenth centuries.[24]

Istrin's edition of *Sermo de obit.* is based on Rome, Biblioteca Vallicelliana, F 33, fols. 61r–66r (16th cent.; =R). Istrin also consulted Paris, Bibliothèque nationale de France, Coislin 121, fols. 53r–55r (14th cent.; =D; lacking 4:11–15 due to damage). Before Istrin, a portion of the text (1:1–4 and 5:6–8) was published by Migne from an unidentified source (*PG* 77:1117–18; =M). There are now twelve extant witnesses of this recension ranging from the ninth to the seventeenth centuries.[25] The earliest manuscript is Vatican, Biblioteca Apostolica Vaticana, Vat. gr. 455, fols. 265r–269r (9th/10th cent.).

In addition to the two Greek recensions, Istrin also published Church Slavonic recensions of both *Mart. Dan.* and *Sermo de obit.*, which resemble but are not fully identical with the corresponding Greek texts. *Mart. Dan.* is taken from the *Great Menaion Reader* produced by Metropolitan Macarius of Moscow, fols. 304r–305v (16th cent.; =Men.).[26] Istrin did not indicate which manuscript he used, but a similar form of the text is found in Moscow, Russian State Library F. 98 #32, fols. 364v–368v (16th cent.) and in F. 98 #59.1, fols. 138–141 (16th/17th cent.). For his edition of *Sermo de obit.* Istrin used Russian State Library, F. 178 #3127, fols. 289v–294v (16th cent.; =SlavR). He also consulted Moscow Theological Academy F.173/I #90, fols. 375v–381r (16th cent.; =SlavM)[27] and Moscow, Russian State Library, V. M. Undolĭskij 560, fols. 83–88 (15th/16th cent.; =SlavU).[28] The text in SlavU follows another homily about Daniel and the Three Youths ascribed to Gregory the monk and presbyter called "A Word of Praise to the Three Youths and Daniel the Prophet" (*Men.*, fols. 331r–336v).[29] In his publication of the Church Slavonic versions of *Mart. Dan.* and *Sermo de obit.*, Istrin

---

24. They are listed in the Pinakes database: https://pinakes.irht.cnrs.fr/notices/oeuvre/15165.

25. https://pinakes.irht.cnrs.fr/notices/oeuvre/12489.

26. See, e.g., Macarius, *Great Menaion Reader*, 11:1093–100. Russian translations of portions of *Men.*, SlavR, SlavZ, UkS, and *Syn. Cp.* are featured in Somov, "Slavonic Tradition," 169–79.

27. This form of the text is also found in *Men.*, fols. 305v–307v; Macarius, *Great Menaion Reader*, 11:1100–107.

28. This collection is now incorporated into Russian State Library, F. 310.

29. Istrin, *Serbian Alexandria*, 185; Macarius, *Great Menaion Reader*, 11:1167–84.

also discusses the links between these two recensions of the *Legend* and several versions of the martyrdom of the synaxarion type, especially those found in the hagiographical book *Prolog* (see below).[30] Moreover, although he originally regarded Church Slavonic *Mart. Dan.* and *Sermo de obit.* as two translations of the same Greek original, he later changed his mind and admitted that the Greek originals of these recensions are different.[31]

Ivan Franko published some other recensions of the *Legend* found in Ukraine that are similar to those of *Mart. Dan.* and *Sermo de obit.*[32] Lorenzo DiTommaso defines them as "Slavonic Legenda Concerning the Three Youths and the Fiery Furnace."[33] These documents are the Church Slavonic Zamość (or "Zamojskyj manuscript"), fols. 753–761 (16th cent.; =SlavZ),[34] housed in the Scientific Library of Ivan Franko National University of Lviv, # 203.III,[35] and a manuscript in Ukrainian of the priest Stephen Teslevtsiv designated Transcarpathia, Shevchenko Institute of Literature of the National Academy of Science of Ukraine, f.3 #769, fols. 105–109, 109–113 (17th/18th cent.; =UkS).[36] SlavZ is similar to *Mart. Dan.* and *Sermo de obit.* but differs from them in some interesting details. UkS contains two texts about Daniel and the Three Youths, but the first one (fols. 105–109) does not contain the legend about their martyrdom. The second version (fols. 109–113) has some details that are absent in SlavZ and represents the martyrdom of Daniel and the Three Youths more schematically, resembling the Synaxarion of Constantinople.

---

30. Istrin, *Serbian Alexandria*, 178–86.
31. Istrin, "Greek Copies," 1.
32. Franko, *Apocrypha and Legends*, 1:307–12.
33. DiTommaso, *Book of Daniel*, 508.
34. Part 1 of the *Legend*, according to the above summary, in this version is close to that in the Krekhiv Palaea (fols. 953–955; 15th/16th cent.). The manuscript is now lost but its contents are described in Franko, *Apocrypha and Legends*, 1:311–12.
35. See more details about SlavZ in Syroyid, "Ancient Kyivan Tales."
36. Stephen Teslevtsiv was a village priest, owner, and possibly compiler of UkS. In his manuscript, Teslevtsiv collected and reworked several legends and apocrypha, usually in the form of homilies; see Franko, *Collected Works*, 260–61. It is difficult to trace how these traditions were transmitted and what texts Teslevtsiv used in writing his compilation. See the description of UkS in Franko, *Carpatho-Russian Literature*, 44–55.

INTRODUCTION

Synaxarion Type

The synaxarion type of the *Legend* is found in the Synaxarion, a liturgical book containing the lives of the saints commemorated according to the church calendar. Usually, Synaxarion entries are shorter versions of an originally longer text. The account of the life and/or martyrdom of a saint who is included in the Synaxarion was to be read at the service dedicated to that saint.

The earliest version of the *Legend* of this type is found in the Synaxarion of Constantinople (*Syn. Cp.*) 317–320 (10th cent.).[37] The first section follows the main story, which basically recounts what is known from the book of Daniel. The story of their martyrdom starts after the conclusion that "they passed away in peace and together with Daniel" (319) with the introductory words: "As some people tell (φασὶ δέ τινες) . . . ." Probably, for the compilers or editors of these texts, the martyrdom account was not seen as contradicting the main narrative but as a natural addition to what is known from the Bible. The martyrdom section recounts that, after the death of King Nebuchadnezzar, Daniel and the Three Youths are arrested, interrogated, and beheaded by a wicked king named Atticus who is persecuting the Jews. They are buried but then their bodies are brought to Mount Gebal by an angel. When Jesus is raised, they are resurrected together with him but then die again soon after.

The same type of story is found in the Menologion of Basil II (*Men. Basil II*), compiled ca. 1000 CE by order of the Byzantine Emperor Basil II (976–1025 CE). Although it is called a menologion, it is in fact an illustrated church calendar with a collection of 430 lives of the saints, each one accompanied by a miniature depicting their martyrdoms.[38] The most representative manuscript is housed in the Bibliotheca Apostolica Vaticana (Vat. gr. 1613).[39] It consists of abridged biographies for the months of September to February and indicates which churches held the relevant commemoration (*synaxis*). The content of this book is, therefore, closer to a synaxarion. Almost every entry is abridged for reasons of format. The text for the Three Youths and Daniel (commemorated 17 December; fols. 251r–252v) is not

---

37. See more detail about the manuscript history of *Syn. Cp.* in Delehaye, *Synaxarium*.

38. See more information about *Men. Basil II* and its manuscripts in Delehaye, "Synaxaire de Sirmond," 404–7.

39. Gianelli, *Codices Vaticani Graeci*, 276–78. The full facsimile of the manuscript was published in Franchi de'Cavalieri, *Menologio di Basilio II*. The Greek with Latin translation is published in *PG* 117:19–614.

an exception; it contains even fewer details than *Syn. Cp*. Their biography is called here ἄθλησις ("contest"), a term often used as a synonym of "martyrdom" in early Christian literature (see *Mart. Tar. Prob. Andr.* 7; *Mart. Theod.* 1.12; *Apos. Con.* 5.1.5).[40] The story is divided into two parts. In the first, Daniel and the Three Youths are carried off into captivity from Jerusalem to Babylon, the Three Youths are delivered from the furnace by the angel, Nebuchadnezzar is honored and blessed by the Lord (cf. Dan 3), and Daniel and the Youths are executed. The second part of the story is about Daniel coming to Babylon from Jerusalem, his prophecy about the birth of the Messiah, his wisdom, fasting, visionary experiences, prophesying, and how he was honored at the court of King Belshazzar (cf. Dan 5:29). A very short account of his martyrdom follows. Later Greek Orthodox liturgical books called Menaia also contain the *Legend*. A Menaion is to be read on Orthodox Matins, sometimes for private reading at home. The *Legend* is found in several printed editions of Greek Menaia[41] in a form similar to that of *Syn. Cp*. Moreover, the Στίχοι ("the verses") preceding this martyrdom account, designed to be read in Matins, directly mention the martyrdom of Daniel and the Three Youths on 17 December.[42]

The Church Slavonic version of the synaxarion type is found in the hagiographical book *Prolog* (Greek πρόλογος, Slavonic *prologŭ*; 12th cent.),[43] whose function is analogous to that of the Synaxarion. In this text, the *Legend* closely resembles the version found either in *Syn. Cp*. (e.g., *Men.*, fols. 337r–337v)[44] or in *Men. Basil II* (*Men.*, fol. 302r).[45] In addition, Dmitry of Rostov includes a version of the *Legend* very similar to that found in *Syn. Cp*. in his *Lives of the Saints* collection (1684–1705). This work is based on the Menologion of Symeon Metaphrastes and on the *Great Menaion Reader* as well as on some other sources, such as the stories collected in the

---

40. Lampe, *Greek Patristic Lexicon*, 46. In the Coptic *Panegyric of the Three Children of Babylon*, the Three Youths are also called "the strong athletes of Christ"; see De Vis, *Homélies Coptes*, 81.

41. For example, Μηναῖον τοῦ Δεκεμβρίου (1863), 115–16; and Μηναῖον τοῦ Δεκεμβρίου (2018), 323–24.

42. See the translation of these Στίχοι in appendix A.

43. Davidova, "Byzantine Synaxarion," 65. For more detail about the relationship between the *Prolog* and the Synaxarion see Istrin, *Alexandria*, 180–83.

44. Macarius, *Great Menaion Reader*, 11:1184–86.

45. Macarius, *Great Menaion Reader*, 11:1085–86.

Introduction

Bollandists' *Acta Sanctorum*. However, in contrast to the Menaion, the lives of these saints were composed for home or private reading.[46]

Several Armenian versions of this type together with English translations have been published by Michael E. Stone. The format and content of the earliest Armenian recension is similar to that of *Syn. Cp.* and *Men. Basil II*. However, it is not a synaxarion in terms of its liturgical use, but is found as the last story in the Lives of the Prophets (together with the stories about Nathan, Elijah, Elisha, and Zechariah) in a Bible manuscript copied by Mekhit'ar of Ayrivank' (ca. 1271–1288): Yerevan, Matenadaran, 1500, fol. 362r (=*Arm.*).[47] In the Armenian tradition, the life of a prophet (*vita*) often follows the book that is ascribed to this prophet. However, in *Arm.*, the Life of Prophets is a single continuous text.[48] Notably, the *Legend* is not incorporated into the larger story of the life of Daniel and the Three Youths but functions on its own. The next Armenian recension of the *Legend* is included in the second edition of the Armenian Synaxarion (*Arm. Syn.²*; 1269) published by G. Bayan.[49] The Armenian Synaxarion is a translation of the Greek Menologion made in 991 CE to which the Armenian saints were added.[50] In *Arm. Syn.²*, Daniel and the Three Youths are commemorated on 9 K'aloc' (17 December). Finally, Stone indicates that the same form of the *Legend* is found in the third recension of the Armenian Synaxarion,[51] while the fourth edition (*Arm. Syn.⁴*; 15th cent.) features another version under the title *Daniel the Prophet and the Three Young Men*[52] that is similar in form to the story found in the manuscript Yerevan, Matenadaran, 1099, fols. 183v–188r (17th cent.).[53] This manuscript contains a miscellaneous series of texts about biblical figures, for example, the Patriarchs, Melchizedek, Job, Moses, Aaron, Elisha, Jeremiah, Ezekiel, and Isaiah, and includes

---

46. There are many editions of this book; see e.g., Dmitry of Rostov, *Lives of the Saints*, 2:128–29.

47. As Stone indicates, it is "an alternative form of material presented in the fourth recension of the Armenian Synaxarion for the feast of these martyrs, drawing on a tradition of Syriac origin" (*Patriarchs and Prophets*, 134). It is not clear whether this Syriac source has survived.

48. Stone, "Armenian Tradition," 111–12.

49. Bayan, "Synaxaire arménien," 65–67.

50. On the complicated history of the Armenian Synaxarion, see Nersessian, "Armenian Hagiography," 458–61; and Mécérian, "Introduction," 99–188.

51. Stone, "Armenian Tradition," 115.

52. Stone, "Armenian Tradition," 116–18.

53. Published in Stone, *Adam to Daniel*, 220–37.

a short account about the martyrdom of the Three Youths as well as the *Inventio* of their relics.[54]

The Chronicle Type

The chronicle type of the *Legend* is a very condensed recension formatted as part of a historical chronicle in Church Slavonic dedicated to the life of Alexander the Great called *Alexandria*. This chronicle was compiled ca. the fifteenth century CE and quickly became popular among south Slavs, Greeks, and Romanians.[55] The second (*Alexandria*²; mid-15th cent.) and the fourth (*Alexandria*⁴; ca. 16th cent.) editions of *Alexandria* briefly describe their martyrdom (2.17). The third edition of *Alexandria* (*Alexandria*³) only briefly mentions the tombs of Daniel and the Three Youths. These texts were published by Istrin.[56]

Title

Since the *Legend* has never been unified, standardized, or harmonized, it has no single title. The *Mart. Dan.* manuscript V published by Istrin is titled Ἀνδραγάθημα καὶ ἄθλησις τῶν ἁγίων τριῶν παίδων καὶ Δανιὴλ τοῦ προφήτου ("The Heroic Deeds and the Contest of the Three Holy Youths and the Prophet Daniel"). Other manuscripts have: Ἄθλησις τῶν ἁγίων τριῶν παίδων Ἀνανία, Ἀζαρία, Μισαὴλ καὶ Δανιὴλ τοῦ προφήτου ("The Contest of the Three Youths Hannaias, Azarias, and Misael, and the Prophet Daniel"; P), and Τοῦ ἐν ἁγίοις πατρὸς ἡμῶν Ἀθανασίου ἀρχιεπισκόπου Ἀλεξανδρείας διήγησις περὶ τῆς ἀθλήσεως τῶν ἁγίων τριῶν παίδων Ἀνανία, Ἀζαρία, Μισαὴλ καὶ Δανιὴλ τοῦ προφήτου ("The Story About the Contest of the Three Holy Youths Hannaias, Azarias, and Misael, and the Prophet Daniel by Our Holy Father Athanasius, the Archbishop of Alexandria"; B).

---

54. The similar tradition of the invention of the relics of the Three Youths is found in Georgian manuscripts from Mount Sinai (10th cent.); see n. 65 below. However, this tradition does not contain the martyrdom.

55. Istrin distinguishes the chronicle *Alexandria* from a novel about Alexander the Great called *Serbian Alexandria* (a translation of Pseudo-Callisthenes' *Alexandria*). *Serbian Alexandria* does not include the *Legend*. For more detail about *Alexandria* in the Church Slavonic tradition, see, e.g., Istrin, *Serbian Alexandria*; Botvinnic, Lourye, and Tvorogov, *Alexandria*; Likhachev et al., *Library*; Milkov, "Directory," 49–51.

56. Istrin, *Alexandria*, 178, appendix 304–5.

Introduction

Istrin's Church Slavonic version *Men.* is called *Moučenïe svętych 3 otrokŭAnanïę Azarïę Misaila i Danïila proroka* ("The Martyrdom of the Three Youths Hannaias, Azarias, and Misael, and the Prophet Daniel").

Sermo de obit. is entitled Τοῦ ἐν ἁγίοις πατρὸς[57] ἡμῶν Κυρίλλου Ἀρχιεπισκόπου Ἀλεξανδρείας λόγος εἰς τὴν τελευτὴν τῶν ἁγίων τριῶν παίδων καὶ τοῦ πανσόφου Δανιήλ ("The Sermon on the Demise of the Three Holy Youths and the All-Wise Daniel by Our Holy Father Cyril, Archbishop of Alexandria") in Istrin's principal manuscript R; D has Τοῦ ἐν ἁγίοις πατρὸς ἡμῶν Κυρίλλου Ἀρχιεπισκόπου Ἀλεξανδρείας λόγος εἰς τοὺς ἁγίους τρεῖς παῖδας καὶ Δανιὴλ προφήτην ("The Sermon of Our Holy Father Cyril, the Archbishop of Alexandria, on the Three Holy Youths and the Prophet Daniel"). In the Church Slavonic version published by Istrin the text is called *Měsęca dekavrïa vŭ 17 Kirila archiepiskopa Aleksandrïiskago slovo na skončanïe svętych trïechŭ otrokŭ i Danïila proroka* ("On 17 December, the Account [=*logos*] of Cyril, the Archbishop of Alexandria, on the Demise of the Three Holy Youths and the Prophet Daniel"). In Macarius's *Great Menaion Reader*, the version ascribed to Gregory the monk and presbyter is entitled *Slovô pochvalïnoe svętymŭ tremŭ ôtrokomŭ i Danïilou prorokou* ("An Account of Praise to the Three Youths and Daniel the Prophet").

In its Synaxarion type, the *Legend* is titled Μνήμη τῶν ἁγίων τριῶν παίδων Ἀνανίου, Ἀζαρίου, Μισαὴλ καὶ Δανιὴλ τοῦ προφήτου ("The Memory of the Three Holy Youths Hannaias, Azarias, Misael, and the Prophet Daniel"; *Syn. Cp.* 317–320), as well as Ἄθλησις τῶν ἁγίων τριῶν παίδων Ἀνανία, Ἀζαρία, καὶ Μισαήλ ("The Contest of the Three Holy Youths, Hannaias, Azarias, and Misael") and Ἄθλησις τοῦ ἁγίου Δανιὴλ τοῦ προφήτου ("The Contest of the Holy Prophet Daniel"; *Men. Basil II*; *PG* 117:212).

The most representative title for the whole story including both the life and deeds of Daniel and the Three Youths in Babylon and their martyrdom and resurrection is that of *Mart. Dan.*: "The Heroic Deeds and the Contest of the Three Holy Youths and the Prophet Daniel." However, in order to use a more compact title that expresses the essence and uniqueness of the *Legend*, this long title is shortened and changed in the present edition to the *Martyrdom of Daniel and the Three Youths*. This is how Istrin refers to it in his edition of the Greek text.[58]

---

57. Istrin appears to have mistakenly read πατρός as πρός in R. D has πατρός. Τοῦ ἐν ἁγίοις πατρὸς ἡμῶν ("of our Holy Father") is the most common formulaic expression in Byzantine literature.

58. Istrin, "Greek Copies," 1.

The Martyrdom of Daniel and the Three Youths

Provenance, Date, Authorship

The origins of the *Legend* cannot be easily established. The earliest manuscripts of *Mart. Dan.* and *Sermo de obit.* are dated from the ninth to the tenth centuries. The shorter version of the *Legend* from *Syn. Cp.* is roughly contemporary as it was likely present in the earliest layers of the text produced by the deacon Euaristus during the reign of Constantine VII Porphyrogenitus (944–959).[59] In general, *Mart. Dan.* and *Sermo de obit.* narrate the same story as *Syn. Cp.*, but there is little lexical or textual dependence between the two narratives and *Syn. Cp.* Moreover, usually Synaxarion texts are an abridged version of a longer story, so it is likely that the form of the text in *Mart. Dan.* and *Sermo de obit.* is closer to the original. However, *Mart. Dan.* and *Sermo de obit.* themselves are far from being identical in their form and manner of presentation.

The *terminus post quem* for the composition of the martyrdom can be derived from several facts. First, both *Mart. Dan.* and *Sermo de obit.* are associated with Alexandria since they are attributed to Cyril of Alexandria (*Sermo de obit.*) and, sometimes, Athanasius of Alexandria (*Mart. Dan.*). These attributions are spurious, but they may relate to the cult of the Three Youths in this city. According to Coptic and Ethiopic tradition, archbishop Theophilus (late 4th cent.) built a church dedicated to the Three Youths in Alexandria. This story is found in the *Life of Saint Abba John the Short* (John Kolobos), who is commemorated on 20 Tekemt.[60] After Theophilus built the church, he asked Abba John to bring the bodies of the Three Youths from Babylon. Abba John was conveyed to Babylon on a cloud and found the tombs of the Youths near that of King Nebuchadnezzar. Abba John spoke to their bodies, asking them to come and dwell in the church dedicated to them in Alexandria. However, the Three Youths declined this invitation because God commanded them to remain in Babylon until the day of the eschatological resurrection (cf. *Mart. Dan.* 5:6). Nevertheless, they ordered that the lighting of the lamps in the church dedicated to them in Alexandria be suspended. In addition, they promised Abba John that they would appear there mystically. After his return to Alexandria, Abba John told all of this to the archbishop. Then, on the night following the consecration of the church, the Three Youths appeared there

---

59. Delehaye, *Synaxarium*, 319–20.

60. *Syn. Alex.* (Basset, 353–54); Budge, *Book of the Saints*, 173–74; and De Vis, *Homélies Coptes*, 121–57.

Introduction

surrounded by brilliant light. They lit all the lamps and sent forth a sweet odor. Theophilus also devoted a sermon to his efforts to acquire the relics (*Sermon on the Three Youths of Babylon*).[61] The church in Alexandria, according to the story, was famous for the Three Youths' power of healing the sick (as reported also in Ps.-Cyril of Alexandria, *Miracles of the Three Youths*).[62] Other accounts, however, make different claims about the fate of the relics. According to the *Vita Sancti Danielis stylitae*, the three saints were brought from Babylon to Alexandria by order of the emperor Leo I (r. 457–474); Euphemius, the patriarch of Constantinople (r. 490–496) deposited them in the tomb of St. Daniel the Stylite.[63] Moreover, patriarch Apollinarius (r. 551–570) may have possessed the hand of one of the Three Youths at Alexandria (Sophronius of Jerusalem, *Vita Cyri et Joannis* 3–5; *PG* 87C:3677–80).[64] Armenian and Georgian traditions say that the relics were discovered in Babylon.[65] Several other texts also report the deposition of Daniel's relics in Babylon (e.g., Epiphanius of Salamis, the *Life of the Prophet Daniel and About His Tomb* [*PG* 43:404–5], and *Arm. Syn.*^{4}.[66] There is also some evidence placing the relics of the Three Youths in Jerusalem,[67] and the existence of a church dedicated to them somewhere in Palestine is indicated by a daily sales record in the Nessana (Auja Hafir) papyri (P.Ness. 90.170, 185; 6th/7th cent.).[68]

All in all, although it is unclear whether the martyrium mentioned by Theophilus ever actually existed (no archeological remains have yet been found), and whether or not this building was related to the later one associated with Apollinarius, the presence of the cult of the Three Youths

---

61. De Vis, *Homélies Coptes*, 124–57.

62. De Vis, *Homélies Coptes*, 160–202.

63. Dawes and Baynes, *Three Byzantine Saints*, 65.

64. Garitte, "Invention géorgienne," 69–70. Antonini suggests that the church of the Three Youths (Τριῶν παίδων [τῶν ἁγίων] νεώς) was built at the time of patriarch Apollinarius ("Chiese cristiane," 164; citing Calderini, *Dizionario*, 177).

65. The *inventio* of the relics of the Three Youths is found in Georgian manuscripts from Mount Sinai (10th cent.) and in Armenian M1099; Garitte, "Invention géorgienne." As Garitte demonstrates, this tradition could relate to some Armenian sources ("Texte Arménien").

66. Cf. Stone, *Adam to Daniel*, 237.

67. Van Esbroeck, "Three Hebrews in the Furnace," 2259.

68. Meimaris, *Sacred Names*, 113; and Kraemer, *Excavations at Nessana*, 269, 276–77, 282–83, 285n170.

The Martyrdom of Daniel and the Three Youths

in Alexandria is well established.[69] In the *Legend*, however, the fate of the relics is rather contradictory: on the one hand, they were in Babylon, on the other, they were hidden on Mount Gebal until their resurrection together with Jesus (both locations are given in 5:5). Moreover, it is unclear what happened to the bodies after their resurrection. They either returned "to their own place" (*Mart. Dan.* 5:10; *Sermo de obit.* is lacunose) or simply soon died again (*Syn. Cp.* 319), but no indication is given where their relics are located. This may indicate that their relics were not in Alexandria or Babylon when the *Legend* was created, and the story about their resurrection was composed to account for their absence.

In addition, *Syn. Cp.* uses the term ἐπιφάνεια (Epiphany) for Nativity (γέννησις) (320).[70] Both feasts were celebrated together as one event until the fourth century CE or even later.[71] It is not clear enough, however, whether this note about Epiphany belongs to the *Legend* itself or to the editor of *Syn. Cp.* Nevertheless, Theophilus's report on the church of the Three Youths, which is evidence of the existence of the cult of these saints in Alexandria, also points to the fourth century. Thus, gathering all these facts together, the *terminus post quem* for the legend about the martyrdom of Daniel and the Three Youths can be defined as around the fourth century.

Furthermore, it is hardly possible to determine with certainty the authorship of the *Legend* as a whole nor of *Mart. Dan.* and *Sermo de obit.*

---

69. Sarrazin, "Three Holy Children," 63–64.

70. Τελεῖται δὲ ἡ αὐτῶν σύναξις ἐν τῇ ἁγιωτάτῃ μεγάλῃ ἐκκλησίᾳ ὧν τὴν μνήμην ἄγειν ὑπὸ τῶν πατέρων ἡμῶν παρελάβομεν πρὸ ἑπτὰ ἡμερῶν τῆς δεσποτικῆς ἐπιφανείας καὶ θείας διὰ σαρκὸς παρουσίας τοῦ κυρίου καὶ Θεοῦ καὶ σωτῆρος ἡμῶν Ἰησοῦ Χριστοῦ ("The liturgical service dedicated to them is commemorated in the Holy Great Church. We have received the instruction from our Fathers to commemorate their memory seven days before the Epiphany of the Master and the divine coming in flesh of our Lord, God, and Savior Jesus Christ") (*Syn. Cp.* 320). This passage is repeated in UkS 3:14, but the term Nativity (*Roždestvo Christovo*) is used instead of Epiphany.

71. In Alexandria the feast of Epiphany was celebrated already in the late second century CE as Clement of Alexandria indicates. He also states that 6 January is the date of Jesus' birth (*Strom.* 1.21.146.1–2); Johnson, "Apostolic Tradition," 65; Bradshaw and Johnson, *Feasts, Fasts and Seasons*, 137. The tradition of celebrating Epiphany on 6 January and including both the themes of birth and baptism of Jesus became common in the church in the last part of the fourth century (Merras, *Feast of Epiphany*, 1). In Alexandria, the feast of the Nativity began to be celebrated on 25 December not later than 432 CE (Buchinger, "Epiphaniefest," 69n13). In Constantinople and Cappadocia the feast of Nativity was celebrated on 25 December from at least 380 CE, but in Jerusalem it was unknown until the fifth century (Bradshaw and Johnson, *Feasts, Fasts and Seasons*, 129–30).

individually, despite their attributions, respectively, to Athanasius and Cyril. Most probably both homilies draw on earlier traditions. For instance, *Mart. Dan.* 3:3 claims to transmit an earlier "extraordinary and completely unknown story" about Daniel and the Three Youths, while *Sermo de obit.* 5:6 refers to an earlier tradition about Daniel that was adopted and incorporated into the homily. In all probability, the origins of the *Legend* are Greek and may go back to some Alexandrian tradition from the early Byzantine period. Although Michael Stone points out that some Syriac source may lie behind the translation of the Armenian version (see below in more detail),[72] it is not clear whether this Syriac source has survived nor whether it was translated from a Greek version of the *Legend*.

Purpose and Possible Audience

The *Legend* mainly developed as a hagiographical narrative and was adapted for liturgical needs. The account of the life and/or martyrdom of a saint included in the Synaxarion was to be read at the service dedicated to that saint, usually in Matins after the sixth ode of the canon. Sometimes it was read in other parts of Matins—for instance, after the seventh ode.[73] The martyrdom of the saint could be read in the church, that is, during the service, while the acts of that saint were read in the refectory.[74] The authors of *Mart. Dan.* and *Sermo de obit.* clearly define the purpose of their homilies not only as honoring the holy martyrs but also as exhorting the members of the church, whether monastic or lay, to follow their righteousness and virtue. For the compilers or editors of these homilies as well as for those of the Synaxarion, the story about the martyrdom of Daniel and his three companions was regarded as a natural addition to what is known from the Bible.[75] Indeed, as DiTommaso states, on the one hand, the story of Daniel in the Hebrew Bible was rapidly accepted as authoritative, but it "neither rendered all the elements of the story inviolate nor suppressed the

---

72. Stone, *Patriarchs and Prophets*, 134.

73. Delehaye, "Synaxaire de Sirmond," 400. In the Evergetis Monastery in Constantinople it could be read after the third ode of the canon (Galadza, "Lives of the Saints").

74. Bovon and Matthews, *Acts of Philip*, 4.

75. Only in some later versions of the *Legend*, which are included in the liturgical books, is it noted that the story is apocryphal and is not found in the Bible. See, e.g., Μηναῖον τοῦ Δεκεμβρίου (1863), 115. Perhaps for this reason, it is excluded from the modern Church Slavonic Menaion.

dynamic process by which the story was continually told and retold."[76] The legendary material about the martyrdom of Daniel and the Three Youths was used only in the context of the narrative of the lives of the saints to give the story greater dramatic and rhetorical effect. Moreover, the textual representatives of the *Legend* never claim any canonical status, though they did claim to use reliable sources (cf. *Sermo de obit.* 5:6). This literature can be categorized not as rejected (apocryphal, in the strict sense of the word), but as useful for encouraging the reader's piety. For this category of literature François Bovon uses the term ψυχωφελής ("useful [profitable] for the soul"), which he adopts from some Byzantine texts.[77] Indeed, in the Eastern Orthodox tradition the term "reading useful for the soul" is often used not only for ascetic monastic literature but also for didactic collections, paterica, lives of the saints, homilies, and even chronicles. Thus, it can be concluded that the *Legend* was intended to be read both for the congregation and for the needs of personal piety.

Genre and Structure

DiTommaso distinguishes between three categories of the Daniel apocryphal literature: legenda, apocalyptica, and prognostica.[78] According to this categorization, *Mart. Dan.* and *Sermo de obit.* belong to Daniel legenda. As DiTommaso defines it, "the legenda are third-person, post-biblical narratives which retell and augment the story of Daniel as it appears in Daniel 1–6"[79] and "are concerned with filling in the gaps in the life and times of Daniel, particularly regarding his early years and his last days, death, and burial."[80] At the same time, the original court tales of Dan 1–6 and their various retellings should be distinguished, because "the latter were also composed in the light of the former."[81] Daniel and his three companions are indeed referred to exclusively in the third person, except in dialogues, and not only in *Mart. Dan.* and *Sermo de obit.* but also in all other types of the *Legend*. And the

---

76. DiTommaso, *Book of Daniel*, 50.

77. Bovon, "Beyond the Canonical," 128. Bovon states the same idea in "'Useful for the Soul,'" 186.

78. As he correctly notes, the distinction between these three categories is rigid; DiTommaso, *Book of Daniel*, 12–14.

79. DiTommaso, *Book of Daniel*, 13.

80. DiTommaso, *Book of Daniel*, 56.

81. DiTommaso, *Book of Daniel*, 50n34.

Introduction

Legend does seek to narrate the origins of Daniel and the Three Youths, their death and burial, and moreover, their resurrection.

In the narrower sense, *Mart. Dan.* and *Sermo de obit.* can be regarded as examples of *vita* in the form in which such texts occur in the Menologion. However, in both *Mart. Dan.* and *Sermo de obit.*, as representatives of the homiletical type of the *Legend*, these traditions were reworked and incorporated into a solemn discourse with a lengthy narrative. As is seen (1:3), they are arranged in the form of a homily intended for spiritual exhortation to be read during Christian worship, usually given after the Scripture readings.

The second half of the *Legend*, featuring the martyrdom of Daniel and his three companions, is structured like a court conflict scenario.[82] It follows the court contest tale literary pattern of persecution and vindication of the righteous found in early Jewish literature, including Dan 3 and 6, and 2 Macc 7[83] (see also Gen 37–45; Isa 52–53; the book of Tobit; the book of Esther; the story of Ahikar; the story of Susanna; Wis 1–6; 3 Macc; 1 En. 62–63; 4 Macc; the Story of Taxo and his seven sons in T. Mos. 9; and some other accounts).[84] The structure of the court conflict scenario can be defined as follows:

1. the situation: the setting of the story, where the main character is in a state of prosperity.
2. the accusation: he or she is endangered.
3. the condemnation: the hero is condemned to prison or even death.
4. the deliverance: he or she is released.
5. the restoration: he or she is vindicated, exalted, and honored.

The structure of the court contest tale is:

---

82. Somov, "Martyrdom of Daniel," 211–25. On the discussion of the genre of the court conflict in Daniel see Humphreys, "Life-Style for Diaspora"; Collins, "Court-Tales"; see also Wright, "Lawsuit of God," 26–67; and Crossan, *Cross That Spoke*, 297–334.

83. While this pattern works well for the full story in Dan 3 and 6, in 2 Macc 7 it is incorporated into each individual account of speech and torture of the seven brothers and their mother; see Crossan, *Cross That Spoke*, 320–21. In addition, the Maccabean martyrs are not delivered from physical death and are not granted a physical deliverance and restoration. Their vindication is postponed as they are promised bodily resurrection and eternal life (the afterlife vindication); see Borg and Crossan, *Last Week*, 166–67.

84. Crossan, *Cross That Spoke*, 301; Nickelsburg, *Resurrection*, 119–40; and Collins, *Commentary*, 39–40.

1. the problem: a person of lower status is called before a person of higher status to be interrogated and to answer difficult questions.
2. the failure: the person of higher status poses a problem which nobody can resolve.
3. the success: the person of lower status can resolve this problem.
4. the reward: this person is rewarded for resolving the problem.[85]

Thus, in the context of this literary plot, the *Legend* is structured as follows:

1. situation: after the death of Nebuchadnezzar and some other kings, a new wicked king from the Persian dynasty named Atticus arises. He arrests Daniel and the Three Youths, puts them to the judgment, and interrogates them.
2. accusation and condemnation: the four are asked about their Jewish religion and their roots. In response, through the mouth of Misael, they rebuke the king for his paganism. Atticus orders the beheading of Daniel and the Three Youths. Then they are martyred.
3. deliverance: the wicked king wants to burn the bodies of the martyred righteous ones after their execution. However, certain pious Jews take their bodies and put them into special silver caskets to bury them. Suddenly, their bodies and heads are miraculously united. After that, the bodies are brought to Mount Gebal by an angel and are hidden there under a rock for 440 years.
4. restoration: at the time of the resurrection of Jesus, they are raised together with him and with many other righteous ones from Israel's past, as well as the repentant bandit (or "Good Thief") who was crucified alongside Jesus. Some of them pass away again until Jesus' second coming, while others go to paradise.

Sources and Literary Unity

The first part of the *Legend* uses several Old Testament books and extra-canonical traditions as sources. The story of the siege and fall of Jerusalem as well as the deportation of the Judeans from Jerusalem to Babylon is based on 2 Kings 24–25, which narrates several sieges of Jerusalem by King

---

85. Collins, *Daniel*, 119; and Crossan, *Cross That Spoke*, 298.

Nebuchadnezzar in the time of kings Jehoiachin and Zedekiah, and LXX Ps 136, which laments the state of the Judean community in Babylon. These two kings of Judah do not appear, however, in the *Legend*. Instead, King Hezekiah is mentioned, who is, according to this story, the father of Hannaias, Azarias, and Misael. In addition, the *Legend* refers to legends about the fall of Jerusalem found in several extracanonical stories about Jeremiah (1:12–13). The details about Jeremiah, Baruch, and Abimelech during Nebuchadnezzar's attack against Jerusalem could have been taken from 4 Baruch (Paraleipomena Jeremiou; early 1st cent.).[86] *Mart. Dan.* and *Sermo de obit.* could have used either the long or the short recension of 4 Baruch,[87] or perhaps an abridged version from the Greek Orthodox Menaion, which collects the legends about Jeremiah for 4 November under the title "The Story About the Lamentation of the Prophet Jeremiah over Jerusalem and About Its Capture and the Trance of Abimelech"),[88] or to the *Tale of the Captivity of Jerusalem*, which is a reworked version of 4 Baruch.[89] Furthermore, the authors of *Mart. Dan.* and *Sermo de obit.* could also be familiar with the *Jeremiah Apocryphon*: an account of the destiny of Jeremiah and Abimelech after the defeat of Jerusalem; it contains many details similar to 4 Baruch.[90] *Jer. Apocr.* is preserved in Coptic and survives also in Arabic and Garšūnī versions as the "History of the Captivity in Babylon." It contains not only the episode about Abimelech's sleep but also some details about the Judeans' march to their captivity in Babylon (*Jer. Apocr.* 30; cf. *Legend* 2:1–4) as well as about the dialogue between the Three Youths and the Babylonians regarding the impossibility of singing psalms in front of the ritually unclean gentiles (*Jer. Apocr.* 33; cf. *Legend* 2:5–6, with reference to LXX Ps 136). The events that take place in Babylon are built on Dan 1–4,[91] blended in with

---

86. Robinson, "4 Baruch," 414.

87. On the long and short recensions of 4 Baruch see Allison, *4 Baruch*, 3–8.

88. See, e.g., Μηναῖον τοῦ Νοεμβρίου, 25–27. This version of the story is similar to the short recension of 4 Baruch (Allison, *4 Baruch*, 5–6). However, the Greek Menaion does not contain the passage about Baruch sitting in the tomb (4 Bar. 4:10–11) to which *Mart. Dan.* and *Sermo de obit.* refer.

89. Turdeanu, "Légende." The Greek text of the *Tale* is in Vassiliev, *Anecdota Graeco-Byzantina*, 308–16; the Church Slavonic is in Tichonravov, *Documents*, 273–83.

90. Text and translation in Kuhn, "Jeremiah Apocryphon."

91. Some details about Daniel in *Syn. Cp.* 317 could be added from the *Vita Danielis* in Liv. Pro.: Daniel was from the tribe of Judah from the family of the special royal service; he was born in upper Beth-horon; he was a temperate man and was considered to be a eunuch (4:1–2). These parallels are textually close to each other. This shows that *Syn. Cp.* knew and used the *Vita Danielis*.

Nebuchadnezzar's vision of the angel/son of God in Th. Dan 3:92 and his vision of a holy watcher in Th. Dan 4:13 (3:8–9).[92]

The sources of the second part of the *Legend* are much less clear. The martyrdom has its unique source, which probably originated in Alexandria. The story of the resurrection of Daniel and the Three Youths is based on Matt 27:52–53 and is designed as an interpretation of this passage. Luke 23:40–43 (the "Good Thief") and 1 Cor 15:6 (the appearance to the 500) are also involved. Furthermore, the deliverance of the patriarchs from Hades and their settlement in paradise indicates familiarity with *Descensus ad inferos* traditions, likely from Egyptian sources but known more widely from the *Gospel of Nicodemus*. In such texts, Jesus liberates Adam and other legendary Hebrew figures from Hades and settles them in paradise. The repentant bandit meets them together with Enoch and Elijah (*Gos. Nic.* 9–10). The bandit's mention of "this word, having removed the flame of fire, brought the bandit to paradise" in *Sermo de obit.* 4:14 alludes not only to Luke 23:40–43 and Gen 3:24, but also to *Gospel of Nicodemus* 10, where the bandit is given a sign of the cross from Jesus as a pass to paradise that he must show to the angel who guards the entrance.

Despite the use of these multiple sources, the text of *Mart. Dan.* represents a literary unity in terms of composition and coherence. *Sermo de obit.* is also a coherent text, except for one important detail in manuscript V, the base text of Istrin's edition. In this manuscript, the account of the resurrection of Daniel and the Three Youths (*Sermo de obit.* 4:11–15) corresponding to *Mart. Dan.* 5:6–9 is misplaced so that they become part of Mishael's answer to King Atticus.

Use of Scripture

Mart. Dan. and *Sermo de obit.* often refer to or allude to the Greek translations of the Hebrew Bible. Most of these references and allusions are made from memory rather than the written biblical text. Some of them are modified and are used as part of creative contextual exegesis, similar to the method of the author of the New Testament Epistle to the Hebrews. For example, in 1:6, the *Legend* "quotes" Isaiah: "Wash yourselves, become clean, and learn to do good. O Jerusalem, in you righteousness lodged, and now murderers! But how does righteousness lodge? The offspring of the

---

92. As noted in the summary, the *Legend* diverges from Dan 4 in having the three youths interpret the dream rather than Daniel.

virgin's flesh" (quoting the version in *Mart. Dan.*). In fact, this "quotation" is a *cento*, collage, or compilation from several loosely used verses from the LXX Isaiah (1:16–17; 1:21; and 7:14). The *Legend* follows with LXX Ps 131:8 and Isa 1:22–23 and ascribes both verses to David: "Rise up, O Lord, into your rest, you and the ark of your sanctity [cf. LXX Ps 131:8]. Your taverners mix the wine with water and your rulers are disobedient" [cf. LXX Isa 1:22–23]. The whole episode about the refusal of the Three Youths to sing psalms in Babylon is based on several verses of LXX Ps 136. Further, the *Legend* ascribes to the prophet Micah: "I will turn your feasts into mourning and I will deport you beyond Babylon" (1:7). However, there is no such text in the book of Micah. In reality the *Legend* is alluding to Amos 5:27 ("and I will deport you beyond Damascus") and 8:10 ("and I will turn your feasts into mourning and all your songs into lamentation").

In both *Mart. Dan.* and *Sermo de obit.* the references and allusions to the book of Daniel are made according to the so-called Theodotion translation (Th.) rather than the Old Greek translation (OG).[93] At an early stage of transmission of Daniel, the OG version was replaced by Th. because it was believed that Th. better resembles the Hebrew text.[94] For instance, Jerome of Stridon states:

> The Septuagint version of Daniel the prophet is not read by the Churches of our Lord and Saviour. They use Theodotion's version, but how this came to pass I cannot tell. Whether it be that the language is Chaldean, which differs in certain peculiarities from our speech, and the Seventy were unwilling to follow those deviations in a translation; or that the book was published in the name of the Seventy, by someone or other not familiar with Chaldee, or if there be some other reason, I know not; this one thing I can affirm—that it differs widely from the original, and is rightly rejected (*Preface to Daniel*; trans. Freemantle).

In fact, both OG and Th. are most probably related to the same Hebrew and Aramaic *Vorlage* (especially in Dan 1–3, 7), but render it differently: the OG is "freer," while Th. is more "literal."[95] Of course, such

---

93. I prefer to use the term OG instead of the LXX in the case of the book of Daniel in order to distinguish between the collection of the Greek texts called the Septuagint as a whole and the original Greek translation of Daniel from the Hebrew Bible and its manuscript traditions, excluding the Theodotion recension. See Tov, *Textual Criticism*, 129; Ross, "Introduction," 5; Screnock, "Septuagint," 135n1.

94. Bledsoe, "Different Editions of Daniel," 179.

95. McLay, *Versions of Daniel*, 4.

characterizations are not types of translation in the modern sense of these terms in the context of translation studies, because all ancient biblical translations were literal enough. The differences between OG and Th. are rather a matter of degree.⁹⁶

Further, there are several references to New Testament texts in the *Legend*. Allusion is made to Jesus' birth from the Virgin as told in Matt 1:25; 2:1 and Luke 2:4–7 (see 3:7); a direct link is made between the resurrection of Daniel and the Three Youths and what happens in Matt 27:52–53 (*Mart. Dan.* 5:6; *Sermo de obit.* 4:11), the passage that describes some spectacular events following the death of Jesus on the cross (heaven shudders, rocks are broken in pieces, the tops of mountains tremble). The number of those resurrected at the crucifixion is given as 500 people in total (*Mart. Dan.* 5:8–9; *Sermo de obit.* 4:13–15). This number is taken from Paul's words in 1 Cor 15:6 about the 500 brethren to whom the resurrected Jesus appeared. In addition, *Sermo de obit.* 4:14 alludes to the episode about the Good Thief (Luke 23:43). Jesus' words "you will be with me in paradise" in Luke 23:43 are transmitted verbatim, omitting only ("today"). The references to Matt 27:53, 1 Cor 15:6, and Luke 23:43 in the *Legend* correspond quite closely to the Greek New Testament; however, they are not direct quotations but rather an example of adaptation, where a reference to a biblical passage exhibits verbal correspondence to the New Testament text but has been adapted to fit a new context.⁹⁷ There are also direct and indirect references to some other New Testament books that are indicated in the commentary below. In addition to quoting biblical material from memory, the authors easily switch between the Bible and various apocryphal traditions.

Theology and Historical Inconsistencies

There are no prominent deviations from mainstream Orthodox dogmatics or Christology in *Mart. Dan.* and *Sermo de obit.* nor in the texts belonging to the other types of the *Legend*. They use the standard christological terms for Jesus: the Son of God (e.g., 3:7), the Word of God (*Mart. Dan.* 4:9; *Sermo de obit.* 4:10), and the "offspring of the Virgin" (*Mart. Dan.* 1:6; cf. 3:7). On the other hand, the term *Theotokos* is not found. The texts prefer παρθένος ("Virgin"; *Mart. Dan.* 1:7) or ἁγνὴ παρθένος ("pure Virgin"; *Mart. Dan.* 3:7). The Trinity (Τριάς) is referred to as παναγία ("the all-holy"),

---

96. Barr, *Typology of Literalism*, 281; and Bons, "Septuagint," 107–8.
97. Osburn, "Methodology," 315.

ὁμοούσιος ("consubstantial") (note to *Mart. Dan.* 3:10), and ἄχραντος ("undefiled") (*Sermo de obit.* 1:3).

The main christological idea reflected in the *Legend* is that it was the Son of God himself who appeared in the furnace with the Three Youths (3:6–9; based on Th. Dan 3:13–23, 91–92). This is how Th. Dan 3:92 (ὁμοία υἱῷ θεοῦ) was interpreted already by Irenaeus. According to him, it was the Word of God (*Haer.* 4.20.11) to be incarnated in Jesus Christ and the Son of God (5.5.2) who appeared in several ways in the Old Testament. Later, this identification of ὁμοία υἱῷ θεοῦ with Jesus Christ, who is the Word of God, occurs in many Christian works (e.g., Hippolytus, *Comm. Dan.* 2.33.4; Tertullian, *Marc.* 4.10.12; 4.21.8; *Prax.* 16.6; Eusebius, *Ecl. proph.* 3.43).[98] Further, ἄγγελος κυρίου ("the angel of the Lord") in Th. Dan 3:49, who is sent to save the Three Youths, is identified by Hippolytus (*Comm. Dan.* 2.32.6–2.34.3) with the μεγάλης βουλῆς ἄγγελος ("The angel of great counsel") in LXX Isa 9:5 and both are taken as references to the Messiah. However, in *Legend* 3:4 and UkS 2:7 it is not simply an angel, but the archangel Michael who is sent by the Lord to the furnace to cool the Three Youths down with water. Moreover, *Mart. Dan.* 3:5 follows some exegetical traditions (e.g., Ephrem the Syrian, *Hymn Fast.* app. 2.10; *Hymn Nat.* 8.6; and *Acta Fruct.* 4.2)[99] in placing the presence of the Holy Spirit in the furnace: "the Spirit of the Almighty Lord was as though He were a moist [wind] whistling on them." Therefore, the *Legend* combines several ideas: an angel cooled the Three Youths, the Son of God appeared to them in the furnace, and the Holy Spirit acted there.

Moreover, according to *Mart. Dan.* 3:7, the Three Youths are aware that the Son of God, whom they see in the furnace, will be incarnated: "We have received every assault on his account, so that when <he who is born according to the> flesh through the pure Virgin comes to us here, as it is written, he may appoint us servants to be martyrs for his sake." It is not clear enough, however, whether they see the incarnated Son of God right in the furnace or later. *Sermo de obit.* 3:7 makes this point more clear: "We endure every assault for his sake, so that when the Messiah comes, he who will be begotten according to the flesh in Bethlehem of

---

98. See Dulaey, "Trois Hébreux," 42–46; Brakmann et al., "Jünglinge im Feuerofen," 364–65.

99. For example: "They were like Hannaias, Azarias, and Misael, so that the divine Trinity was visible also in them. For to each at his post in the flames the Father was present, the Son gave his aid, and the Holy Spirit walked in the midst of the fire" (*Acta Fruct.* 4.2; trans. Musurillo, ed.).

Judea, he who appeared in the thornbush, by means of our kinswoman according to what was predicted in the Law, as our blessed mother taught us, then passing on, we will be among the martyrs brought to him." Here, the Lord's appearance to Moses in the burning bush (Exod 3:2–14) and the Son of God's appearance to the Three Youths in the furnace are both examples of Old Testament Christophany. This was a widespread christological idea in early Christian and patristic exegesis.[100]

Thus, in *Sermo de obit.* 3:7, the incarnation clearly takes place when Christ is born in Bethlehem. This supports the idea that the Son of God's presence in the furnace foreshadows his presence in the womb of the Virgin Mary and that the manifestation in the furnace is a real encounter with Christ to be incarnated.[101] The *Legend* needs these ideas to explain why those who had never seen Christ became martyrs for his sake—because they see him in the furnace as the one to be incarnated, and because he appointed them there to be his witnesses. Therefore, Daniel and the Three Youths suffer not only for their adherence to the Mosaic law, but for Christ, whom they saw in the fiery furnace. They are considered Christian martyrs.

In addition, the resurrection of Daniel and the Three Youths is directly related to the resurrection of Jesus and connects the resurrection of these righteous ones with Matt 27:45–53 and 1 Cor 15:6. The miracle of joining their heads to their bodies (5:4; *Syn. Cp.* 319) may prefigure their future resurrection. Similarly, the uncovering of the rock on Mount Gebal, under which the bodies of the martyrs are hidden (5:5; *Syn. Cp.* 319), may allude to the splitting of the rocks at their resurrection as in Matt 27:51. Moreover, the resurrection of Daniel and the Three Youths as well as other righteous people in *Mart. Dan.* 5:6–9 and *Sermo de obit.* 4:11–15 is a fusion of the belief in bodily resurrection and the temporary restoration of physical life. Probably this is because this tradition takes only the resurrection of Jesus as the unique resurrection to eternal life before the end of time,[102] as Paul states, "for as all die in Adam, so all will be made alive in Christ. But each in his own order: Christ the first fruits, then at his coming those who belong to Christ" (1 Cor 15:22–23).

Therefore, although the resurrection of the righteous ones is a bodily one (*Mart. Dan.* 5:6; *Sermo de obit.* 4:11) and happens together with the

---

100. Bucur, *Scripture Re-Envisioned*, 82–100. See references to the examples of this interpretation in the commentary on *Sermo de obit.* 3 below.

101. Bucur, "Christophanic Exegesis," 240.

102. Somov, "Martyrdom of Daniel," 225.

resurrection of Jesus, the two events have different features. After resurrection, Daniel and the Three Youths go to paradise either in corporeal or incorporeal form. Such an uncertainty about the state of the resurrected ones could have been inherited by this tradition from the ambiguity of the destiny of the risen saints in Matt 27:52–53. This passage has a long history of interpretation. For instance, Ignatius of Antioch states that the saints in Matt 27:52–53 are the Old Testament prophets (*Magn.* 9.2). Clement of Alexandria connects Matt 27:52–53 with Jesus' descent into hell to deliver the righteous and declares that the resurrected saints are those righteous who ascended from there together with Jesus (*Strom.* 6.6.47–48).[103] The *Gospel of Nicodemus* also links the descent to Matt 27:52–53. In this tradition, the risen saints are much more personalized, and we know the names of two of them: Karinus and Leucius, according to the Latin version of this text (17:3). They are two sons of the high priest Simeon, who received the child Jesus in his arms in the temple (Luke 2:25–35). The reason they are raised is because they had to testify about what Jesus did there. Notably, according to the story, Karinus and Leucius disappear from the world of the living after delivering their narrative, since they were allowed to spend only three days there. Similarly, in UkS the risen Daniel and the Three Youths not only appear to many people but also "spoke to all who saw them" (3:13).

In addition, it is unclear whether paradise, where some resurrected righteous ones are sent by the Lord (*Mart. Dan.* 5:8; *Sermo de obit.* 4:13), is a place reserved for the righteous before their future resurrection or it is their final blessed destination. The idea of eschatological paradise is based on the prophecies of the Hebrew Bible about the restoration of Israel (Isa 51:3; Ezek 36:33, 35), which is patterned on the model of primeval Eden (Gen 2:8–10; cf. Ezek 28:13; 31:8).[104] In 1 Enoch paradise is an earthly realm (32:3–4; 77:3), but in 2 Enoch it is a heavenly abode of the righteous located on the third level of the heavens (2 En. 8:1–10). In some early Christian texts, the final abode of the righteous (e.g., Rev 22:1, 5) and the kingdom of God (*Apoc. Pet.* 16; *Mart. Perp. Felic.* 4.22, 26; 11.11, 15) are represented as a paradise-like garden. Moreover, Tertullian thought that Christian martyrs go directly to paradise immediately after death (*An.* 55.4; cf. *Mart. Pol.* 14.2), whereas Gk. Apoc. Ezra 1:12; 5:20–22 and Vis. Ezra 58–59, 64 depict paradise as a temporary place for the reward of the righteous before their

---

103. For other texts detailing Jesus' descent into hell, see Somov, "Martyrdom of Daniel," 221–24.

104. Somov, *Representations of the Afterlife*, 91.

resurrection and the final judgment at the end of time.[105] Such an ambiguity about paradise persists in both *Mart. Dan.* and *Sermo de obit*.

On the whole, the *Legend* is not very thorough in historical detail (as derived from the Bible) and contains some anachronisms. Thus, it regards Nebuchadnezzar not only as a Babylonian king but also as king of Assyria (e.g., 1:8),[106] mixing the reign of Hezekiah (8th cent. BCE) and that of Zedekiah (6th cent. BCE).[107] Accordingly, it is surprising that the Three Youths are children of Hezekiah, who lived several hundred years earlier (4:8).[108]

Furthermore, the persecutor of Daniel and the Three Youths, named Atticus (4:1), cannot be identified with any historical Persian ruler of the time. In Armenian tradition Atticus was a king after Artashes (Artaxerxes?) (*Arm. Syn.*[4]) or even Cyrus (*Arm.*). In the Church Slavonic *Life of Daniel and the Three Youths* by Dmitry of Rostov, this king is identified as Cambyses—probably Cambyses II (530–522 BCE), a son of Cyrus, and also with Artaxerxes.[109] It is uncertain, however, which Artaxerxes he has in mind—Artaxerxes I (465–424 BCE), Artaxerxes II (404–358 BCE), or Artaxerxes III (404–338 BCE). In *Mart. Dan.* 4:6 Atticus's father is named Magedon, but this name is not associated with any Persian kings either. The details of his life given here ("being in companionship with Syrians, lusted for a marriage") do not help us to trace his origins; the meaning of this name is also uncertain.[110]

In Misael's controversy with Atticus, the king is rebuked for his Manichaeanism (*Mart. Dan.* 4:7; *Sermo de obit.* 4:5). This is historically inconsistent, since Manichaeans did not appear until the third century CE. Therefore, the existence of the Manichaeans in Persia at the time of Daniel and the Three Youths is an obvious anachronism. Moreover, their characteristics (listed in *Mart. Dan.* 4:7) are completely fallacious and are rather a mixture of popular prejudice and several folkloristic tropes.

---

105. Somov, "Martyrdom of Daniel," 225.

106. A similar anachronism is found in the book of Judith: "It was the twelfth year of the reign of Nebuchadnezzar, who ruled over the Assyrians in the great city of Nineveh" (Jdt 1:1). Probably, it is a composite image of the world empire, which is the enemy of Israel.

107. Moreover, the nightly feast at Jerusalem, which precedes the beginning of the siege of the city by Babylonians, is described as a pagan orgy (1:10–11).

108. Though, some other Christian traditions about Daniel and the Three Youths also offer strange genealogies (see the commentary below).

109. Dmitry of Rostov, *Lives of the Saints*, 128.

110. See the commentary on *Mart. Dan.* 4:6 below for more detail.

Introduction

The *Legend* also bears traces of polemics against several other heretical groups: Pneumatomachi, Magusaeans, and Macedonians (see the notes to *Mart. Dan.* 4:7 and SlavZ 4:6). SlavZ may even allude to the names of some heresiarchs: Macedonius I of Constantinople and Atticus of Constantinople (4th/5th cent.). The arguments of the polemic in SlavZ are odd and have little or nothing to do with the teachings of these groups. Nevertheless, the anti-heretical polemic is apparently intended to testify to this tradition's adherence to Orthodox doctrines.[111]

Christian, Jewish, and Anti-Jewish Elements

Apart from obvious Christian elements in the *Legend* that concern dogmatics and Christology, there are also some Jewish elements that can be discerned in this story. For instance, King Atticus's interrogation of Daniel and the Three Youths concerns their Jewish origin and aspects of their Jewish beliefs ("Jewish wisdom"), rather than their vision of Christ in the fiery furnace (4:2). Thus, the story of the trial of these righteous ones is reminiscent not only (and not so much) of acts of Christian martyrdom, but also the interrogation and execution of the Maccabean martyrs who did not submit to the Syrian king Antiochus IV Epiphanes (2 Macc 7; 4 Macc).

In addition, the Israelites who were captives in Babylon carried away the bodies of the martyrs, mourned over them, and made coffins for their burial (5:4). Their bodies were then carried to Mount Gebal, which is identified with the mountain in Samaria that played a special role in the biblical account of Israel's exodus from Egypt. This may imply that the four righteous ones were carried to their homeland even before the people of Israel returned there from captivity.

Furthermore, although the *Legend* does not include explicit polemical arguments against Judaism and is not to be regarded as an anti-Jewish treatise or a special homily *adversus Judaeos*,[112] it does reflect some typical Christian presuppositions against Judaism and contains some clear anti-Judaic elements. The most prominent one is that the Jews are those

---

111. The fact that *Mart. Dan.* and *Sermo de obit.* are found in manuscripts that contain homilies and commentaries attributed to such orthodox authors as John Chrysostom, Basil of Caesarea, Andrew of Crete, or John of Damascus also indicates that the *Legend* was considered quite consistent with orthodox theology.

112. On this genre of Christian literature see, e.g., Williams, *Adversus Judaeos*; Ruether, "Adversus Judaeos," 27–50; and Albl, "Ancient Christian Authors," 18–21.

who carried out the crucifixion of Jesus: "When the Jews set up the Cross against our Lord Jesus Christ" (*Mart. Dan.* 5:6). This is the typical Christian accusation of the Jews for the death of Jesus on the cross going back to 1 Thess 2:14–15. Many Christian writers make the Jews fully responsible for Jesus' death (e.g., Justin, *Dial.* 17.1; Eusebius, *Dem. ev.* 1.1.7; Lactantius, *Inst.* 4.10.18; Augustine, *Adv. Jud.* 7.10; John Chrysostom, *Adv. Jud.* 1.7.2, 5).[113] In addition, in *Mart. Dan.* and *Sermo de obit.*, the Jews of Jesus' time are contrasted with those living at the time that Daniel and the Three Youths were martyred: those who crucified Christ are οἱ Ἰουδαῖοι (Jews), while those who mourned for Daniel and the Three Youths are οἱ Ἑβραῖοι (Hebrews; 3:1; 4:1–2), οἱ υἱοὶ Ἰσραήλ (the children of Israel; 5:5; *Sermo de obit.* 4:1), ὁ λαὸς Ἰσραήλ (the people of Israel; *Sermo de obit.* 5:4), or simply Ἰσραήλ (Israel; *Mart. Dan.* 5:4; *Sermo de obit.* 4:10). Thus, *Mart. Dan.* and *Sermo de obit.* follow the typical Christian idea that the Jews of Jesus' time rejected him as the messiah and are responsible for his death. Unlike many early Christian accounts, however, which portray the history of Israel as a chain of numerous rebellions against God, rejections and killings of God's prophets (Justin, *Dial.* 39.1; *Barn.* 5.11; Lactantius, *Inst.* 4.11.3; John Chrysostom, *Adv. Jud.* 5.9.5),[114] the martyrdom of Daniel and the Three Youths is more positive about Israelites and depicts them as people faithful to their Lord. Thus, they were committed to their faith and did not follow pagan beliefs even after three kings had reigned in Babylon after their resettlement there (3:1); they mourned the death of Daniel and his three companions, built gold coffins for them, and hid them from the wicked pagan king who wanted to burn their bodies (5:4–5).

Iconography of the Martyrdom of Daniel and the Three Youths

One of the widespread iconographical images of the prophet Daniel is based on the narrative of Dan 6 and portrays him as being delivered from the den of lions. This composition was known from early Christian times (e.g., the fourth-century catacombs of St. Januarius in Naples) and was interpreted as the typology of Christ being in the tomb. The Three Youths are often depicted in the context of Dan 3. Usually, two scenes from this chapter of Daniel are depicted: (1) the appearance of the Three Youths before

113. Albl, "Ancient Christian Authors," 41–43.
114. Albl, "Ancient Christian Authors," 43–44.

Introduction

Nebuchadnezzar who interrogates them or points out the idol to venerate; (2) their imprisonment in the fiery furnace and rescue by the angel.[115] These images occur in catacombs, in mosaics, and on sarcophagi and icons. The scene from Dan 3 is found already in frescoes of the Roman catacomb of Priscilla (2nd/3rd cent.).[116] The iconography of this story is ambiguous in its way of representing the imagery of the fourth figure in the furnace, which sometimes occurs in the composition: it is either an angel, or the archangel Michael, or even directly Jesus Christ.[117]

While Daniel and the Three Youths' salvation from death is common imagery in the iconography of these righteous ones, the iconographical tradition about their martyrdom is not widespread. It is found in *Men. Basil II*, for instance.[118] Almost every story in this Menologion is illustrated by a miniature that reflects the main points of the narrative. The story of the Three Youths and Daniel is illustrated by two pictures. Each of them portrays an episode from the biblical text and then the martyrdom (Vat. gr. 1613, fols. 251r–252v). The first miniature depicts the angel of the Lord rescuing the Three Youths from the furnace and their decapitations. The fourth figure in the furnace is depicted as an angel placing his hands on two of the three young men and delivering them all from the fire. The second miniature illustrates Daniel in the lions' den and his decapitation. These miniatures are a prominent example of the attestation of the martyrdom of Daniel and the Three Youths, not only at the textual level but also in iconography.

In addition, Daniel and the Three Youths sometimes appear in the iconography of Christ's descent into hell. This imagery is found, for example, in the manuscript of Vatican, Biblioteca Apostolica Vaticana, Urb. gr. 2, fol. 260v (1122); on the Russian icon of Christ's descent into hell from Pskov (15th cent.) located in the Russian State Museum, St. Petersburg; on the icon by Daniel Cherny and Andrei Rublev (1425–1427) from the iconostasis of the Trinity Lavra of St. Sergius; and on that by Dionisius the Wise (1502) from the iconostasis of the Ferapontov Monastery, located in the Russian State Museum. The Three Youths can be recognized there as three young

---

115. Brakmann et al., "Jünglinge im Feuerofen," 375–84; Rassart-Debergh, "Biblical Subjects," 389.

116. Bucur, "Christophanic Exegesis," 230.

117. Bucur, "Christophanic Exegesis," 230–31.

118. Vat. gr. 752 (the Byzantine book of Psalms; 11th cent.) does not depict the martyrdom but the Three Youths are in the furnace wearing martyrs' crowns.

men with caps. This imagery goes back to Dan 3:21: "So the men were bound, still wearing their tunics, their trousers, their hats, and their other garments, and they were thrown into the furnace of blazing fire."

Translation

The language of *Mart. Dan.* and *Sermo de obit.* published by Istrin is Byzantine Greek with some rhetorical elements typical of homilies. There are certain orthographic peculiarities indicating the phonetic characteristics of that period,[119] but also outright misspellings.[120] These two Greek recensions have never been translated into any European language.[121] The present translation of the *Martyrdom of Daniel and the Three Youths* is an annotated translation of the Greek recensions of the *Legend* based on Istrin's diplomatic Greek editions in consultation with several earlier surviving Greek manuscripts available to me (P, B, C, and D), the Church Slavonic recensions published by Istrin (*Men.*; SlavR; SlavM; SlavU), and the two versions from Ukraine published by Franko (SlavZ and UkS). For the most part, the translations follow Istrin's main texts unless there is compelling reason to substitute variant readings from his critical apparatus; based on the assumption that both texts have a common ancestor, for *Mart. Dan.* this means when a variant reading agrees with *Sermo de obit.* (sometimes with SlavZ), and for *Sermo de obit.* when a variant reading agrees with *Mart. Dan.* The reader should be cautioned that Istrin's edition of *Sermo de obit.* is deeply flawed as it relies on two problematic manuscripts: the pages of R are out of order and material in parallel with *Mart. Dan.* 5:6–9 is displaced, and D has a lacuna in 4:11–15 due to damage. In addition, Istrin does not report all of the variants in D. Certainly a new edition is a desideratum. In order to give the reader a fuller understanding of the further development of the *Legend*, included also are translations of several other Greek, Church Slavonic, and Ukrainian texts arranged in two appendices. Appendix A features the translation of the synaxarion and chronicle types of

---

119. Most phonetic peculiarities are due to the interchange between ει-ι and οι-ι in Byzantine Greek as a result of so-called iotacism—e.g., καλλίκλαδοι instead of καλοὶ κλάδοι (*Sermo de obit.* 1:4); εἴρ instead of ιρ (3:8–9); ἴδομεν instead of εἴδομεν (4:16).

120. E.g., φιλαπτόριον (*Sermo de obit.* 5:1) instead of φιβλατόριον ("cloak," cf. *Mart. Dan.* 5:1); ἐνήχει instead of ἐν ἤχει ("with a sound"; *Mart. Dan.* 1:14).

121. Istrin provides only a brief paraphrase close to the text of the Church Slavonic *Sermo de obit.* he published (*Serbian Alexandria*, 183–84).

the martyrdom: the passages from *Syn. Cp.* (317–320), *Men. Basil II* (PG 117:212), the Στίχοι ("the verses") from the Greek Orthodox Menaion on 17 December, as well as the short account on the martyrdom of Daniel and the Three Youths from *Alexandria*² 2.17 and *Alexandria*⁴ 2.17. Appendix B features the translations of SlavZ and UkS.

The translation technique I use is a balanced approach between functional dynamic translation, which seeks to convey the meaning of the original text, rather than its form, and a more literary scholarly translation, which tries to preserve the features of the original and maintains some cultural-historical distance, but without artificial archaization.

Chapter divisions for *Mart. Dan.* and *Sermo de obit.* are adopted from Istrin's edition; however, the versification and section divisions are my own and are based on the semantic and literary structure of the text, and on the consistency between them. The division into chapters and versification in the translation of SlavZ takes *Mart. Dan.* as a pattern, but chapters and versification in UkS are again my own, made according to its semantic, literary, and thematic structure as well as its consistency with other versions of the *Legend*. When the *Legend* quotes or refers to the LXX, I generally follow the second printing of *A New English Translation of the Septuagint* (NETS), slightly adapted in some cases.

The Heroic Deeds and the Contest of the Three Holy Youths and the Prophet Daniel

1 ¹Thus, I would like, beloved ones, to set out in detail a good and virtuous guidance to the churches of Christ about the heroic deeds^A of Christ's Youths and martyrs. So, as much as you know God—more so, you are known by him—then, by lending^B me your ears, listen, so that you can be deemed worthy of the reward of the martyrs about whom it will be spoken. ²For those people who have not seen them should praise and marvel at those who have accepted martyrdom—namely, those who became his confessors and witnesses^C of the death and resurrection from the dead even before Christ's glorious coming in flesh.^D ³It is not we who proclaim to you about them, but it is the foresight of the

Gal 4:9

A. *the heroic deeds*: ἀνδραγάθημα ("brave," "virtuous," "heroic" deeds). This can relate either to the first part of the *Legend*, which narrates their life in Babylon, or to both to their life and martyrdom. The related noun ἀνδραγαθία is sometimes used in the LXX in the context of the Maccabean revolt (1 Macc 1:56; 9:22; 10:15; 16:23; 2 Macc 14:18). Moreover, in 4 Macc 1:8 this term refers to the martyrdom of Eleazar as well as the seven brothers and their mother.

B. *lending*: προτείναντες. C has the imperative (προτείνατε).

C. Probably, the author is playing with two meanings of μάρτυρ: witness and martyr.

D. The author directly indicates that he regards Daniel and the Three Youths as martyrs not only for their faithfulness to the Jewish law but first for their adherence to Christ.

prophecy that has just been read to us[A] that is speaking.[B] ⁴For this reason, I also would like to describe the good way of life and the death of the kingly and kindred[C] Youths Hannaias, Azarias, and Misael, together with the all-wise and divine man[D] Daniel. Come now, let us set[E] the cornerstone of the ancient building, for which reason the most beautiful[F] Youths of Jerusalem were settled as bastions at the ends of the world.

⁵What do I set forth before you, Jerusalem? How shall I praise its own acts and way of life?[G] Accusing,[H] I shout at you but advocating, I marvel at the word, which as a command God has spoken to you up to four times, testifying and saying through David, "*If his[I] sons forsake my law and by my judgments do not walk.*" ⁶He also commands through Isaiah, "*Wash yourselves, become clean* (and) *learn to do good.* O Jerusalem, *in you righteousness lodged, and now murderers!* But how does righteousness lodge?[J] *The offspring of the virgin according to the flesh*," which also David, foreseeing, cries, "*Rise up, O Lord, into your rest, you and the ark of your sanctity. Your taverners mix the wine with water and your rulers are disobedient.*"[K] ⁷[The Lord] also says through Micah, "*I will turn your feasts into mourning and I will deport you beyond Babylon.*"[L]

LXX Ps 88:31

LXX Isa 1:16–17, 21
Isa 7:14

LXX Ps 131:8
LXX Isa 1:22–23
Amos 5:27; 8:10

    A. *the prophecy . . . read to us*: this may relate to the scriptural reading, which was appointed for the feast of Daniel and the Three Youths, likely 17 December, according to the Eastern Orthodox Church calendar. However, it is not easy to define which portion from the Scriptures was read. In modern practice, there are no special readings on this day dedicated to these saints. Probably, Dan 3 was read.

    B. *is speaking*: BC have "that we proclaim."

    C. *kindred*: Men. has "their church kinsmen."

    D. *divine man*: lacking in PB.

    E. *let us set*: ἐνστησώμεθα. PBC have ἀναστησώμεθα ("let us raise up").

    F. *most beautiful*: κάλλιστοι. C has καλλίνικοι ("the gloriously triumphant").

    G. *how shall I praise . . . life* (PBC SlavZ cf. *Sermo de obit.*): V has the truncated phrase "about what way of life."

    H. V inserts "not."

    I. *his*: PBC have "your" (cf. SlavZ).

    J. *and now . . . lodge*: added from P (cf. *Sermo de obit.* and SlavZ).

    K. Although this "quotation" continues "David's words," here the author switches to Isaiah and quotes Isa 1:22–23.

    L. This "quotation" is absent in Micah. However, the first portion is from

The Heroic Deeds and the Contest

⁸Because you persisted in disobedience,^A he now prepares against you the king of Assyria in remembrance of the treasure of Hezekiah; he stands against you.^B ⁹For he made no mistake, choosing men mighty in strength and experienced in war and horses both swift and furious in battles, on which were mounted younger mighty ones equipped with armor; and with both hands throwing out javelins, they did not miss.^C ¹⁰Then, Nebuchadnezzar the king of Babylon attacked the city^D at the third hour of the night. For there was a great feast in the city at that time^E and a torchlit procession, dances, and drunken parties, cymbals, and lyres as well as the stomping of those who were dancing. ¹¹Neither the nobles nor the free people were away from the city;^F every assembly gathered^G from the different classes of people and were equally engaged in the drunken parties.^H ¹²But^I Jeremiah

2 Kgs 18:13–16; Isa 36:1

2 Kgs 25:1; Hab 1:6–10; Dan 1:1

Amos 8:10 and the second recalls Amos 5:27: "and I will deport you beyond Damascus." In *Sermo de obit.*, SlavZ, and *Men.* this quotation is also ascribed to Micah.

A. P has: "and you did not persist in obedience."

B. *in remembrance . . . against you*: added from PBC (cf. *Sermo de obit.* and SlavZ). PB follow with "having turned back the king of Assyria," which may be an error due to dittography. The "treasure" likely refers to the ransom paid by Hezekiah (r. 716–687 BCE) to Sennacherib of Assyria in exchange for his withdrawal from Jerusalem.

C. V adds "their target" (lacking in PBC and SlavZ).

D. V adds "Jerusalem" (lacking in PBC and SlavZ).

E. *great feast in the city at that time*: PBC have simply "feast"; SlavZ "great feast."

F. *neither . . . city*: the reading here is based on PBC due to their agreement with *Sermo de obit.* and SlavZ. V has: οὐκ εὐγενὴς ὅτε οὐδεὶς παρετεῖτο τῆς πόλεως οὐκ ἐλεύθεροι οὐ δοῦλοι οὐ παῖδες οὐ παιδίσκαι ("not the nobles, at the time no one was away from the city, not the free ones nor the slaves, nor the boys, nor the girls").

G. *every assembly gathered* (PBC cf. *Sermo de obit.*): V has "but every generation and every assembly."

H. This picture of the behavior of the inhabitants of Jerusalem, similar to pagan orgies, seems to be intended to show that because of their disobedience they had completely lost the watchfulness to which God often calls believers (cf. Mark 13:32–37; Luke 21:34–36; 1 Thess 5:3–7). In addition, the dances at this feast may allude to Lam 5:15 (cf. also LXX Ps 54:11, "lawlessness and trouble are within it").

I. V adds "only."

LXX Jer 29:6;
MT Jer 47:6
4 Bar. 4:7–12

was running around,^A lamenting, saying,^B *"How long until you will be quiet, O God?"*^C ^13And the prophet Baruch^D got angry, being locked in the chasm^E on account of their lawless deed,^F and the prophet Abimelech kept watch outside the city^G in order

> A. According to 4 Bar. 4, Jeremiah, Baruch, and Abimelech are led in different directions at the destruction of Jerusalem. Baruch and Abimelech were promised a deliverance from death during the destruction of Jerusalem (Jer 39:16–18; 45:2–5).
>
> B. *saying*: lacking in B.
>
> C. In its original context this prophecy is addressed to the Philistines "before Pharaoh attacked Gaza" (MT Jer 47:1). This could happen either in 601 BCE when the battle of Pharaoh Necho with Nebuchadnezzar took place or when this Pharaoh Necho came to defeat and slay Josiah at Megiddo (2 Kgs 23:29, 30; cf. Herodotus, *Hist.* 2.159) in 609 BCE as he moved north. See Thomson, *Book of Jeremiah*, 696–97.
>
> D. In the final form of 4 Baruch, Baruch is portrayed as a more important and independent figure, i.e., a prophet, and scribe rather than simply an assistant of Jeremiah from the canonical book of Jeremiah (cf. Jer 36:4). See Robinson, "4 Baruch," 415.
>
> E. According to 4 Bar. 4:12, Baruch was sitting not in the chasm but in a tomb, where he spent sixty-six years (cf. 5:2; 6:2). Therefore, the chasm may allude to the tomb, which the prophet entered, whereas his lock may correspond to the long period of sixty-six-year sleep of Abimelech. This tradition is traced back to 2 Bar. 21:1, where Baruch is sitting and mourning in a cave in the valley of Kidron.
>
> F. *their lawless deed*: C has "the disorder."
>
> G. *outside the city*: lit. "in a field" (ἐν ἀγρῷ). In 4 Bar. 3:12–13 Abimelech is identified with Abdemelech (Αβδεμελεχ in LXX Jer 45:7), the Ethiopian who was a eunuch in the house of King Zedekiah in Jerusalem. In some LXX manuscripts, however, the name is changed to Ἀβιμέλεχ, which is the much more widely used form of the name in the Bible (cf., e.g., Gen 20–21; 26:1, 8–11, 16, 26; Judg 8:31; 9:1–6, 16–56; 10:1; 2 Sam 11:21; 1 Chr 18:16; Ps 34:1). Probably 4 Baruch also intends to fit this name to that one (see Herzer, *4 Baruch*, 66). Abimelech helped to save Jeremiah from the cistern in which he was thrown (Jer 38:6–13). Then he was promised that he will see the destruction of Jerusalem but will be delivered from death (39:16–18). In 4 Baruch, Jeremiah recalls Abimelech's help and the Lord's promise to save him (4 Bar. 3:12–13). The Lord commands Jeremiah to send Abimelech to the vineyard of Agrippa until the end of the Exile (3:14). Then, Jeremiah asks Abimelech to go to the farm (χωρίον) of Agrippa to get some figs for the sick (3:21–22). There he will spend sixty-six years sleeping under a tree. The exact location of this place is problematic (see the discussion in Herzer, *4 Baruch*, 68–78), but it is clear that it was sufficiently far from Jerusalem. *Mart. Dan.* and *Sermo de obit.* paraphrase this story replacing ἀμπελών (4 Bar. 3:10) and χωρίον (3:15; 5:25) with ἀγρός. The main idea remains the same: Abimelech is

not to see the desolation of the city and the misfortune that suddenly occurred. ¹⁴When the king of the Babylonians^A appeared, buzzing trumpets in seven ranks echoed out with a great and low mechanical^B sound. Fiery iron wheels,^C spinning around, quickly crushed the walls, leveling them down and crushing them.^D ¹⁵The pounding of chariots . . . warriors' quivers clashed together,^E and the furious^F horses, whinnying with a barbaric noise, gnashed loudly.^G ¹⁶And^H both produced a violent thunder, so that the drunken party was immediately^I hidden away and the torches were extinguished—as the prophet said, "*to turn their feasts into mourning and their joy^J into lamentation.*" (There were) in that place^K collapsed walls, destruction,^L burning, and a confusion of corpses at the temple. ¹⁷And the sacred equipment for worship, which was a countless value of gold,^M and everything that was captured were brought out from that unjust act.^N

4 Bar. 3:15–16; 5:1–2

Josh 6:16

2 Kgs 25:10; Jer 52:14

LXX Amos 8:10
2 Kgs 24:10—25:17; 2 Chr 36:17–20; Jer 52:13–23; Dan 1:2

---

safe and far away from the destruction of Jerusalem.

A. V adds "suddenly" (lacking in PBC and SlavZ).

B. *mechanical*: μιχανικῇ. B has μανικοί ("furious").

C. *fiery iron wheels*: "wheels" is supplied by PBC (cf. *Sermo de obit.* and SlavZ).

D. *crushing them*: lacking in PB.

E. *the pounding . . . clashed together* (cf. *Sermo de obit.*): the reading here is a (still problematic) reconstruction based on *Sermo de obit.* V provides ἡ τύπτος ἁρμάτων ("the pounding of chariots") followed by βαρὺς ἀνεκρούετο ("heavy clashed"); PBC provide ἡ ἁρμάτων βαρὺς φαρέτραι πολεμιστῶν συνεκρούοντο ("the heavy chariots, warriors' quivers clashed together").

F. *furious*: μανικοί. C has πολεμικοί ("hostile").

G. *proudly*: ὑψιμελῶς (from ὑψηλῶς) in PB (cf. *Sermo de obit.*). C lacks "gnashing proudly." V has "loudly."

H. *and*: P has "as."

I. *immediately* (PBC cf. *Sermo de obit.*): lacking in V.

J. *their joy*: τὴν χαράν. LXX Amos 8:10 has πάσας τὰς ᾠδὰς ὑμῶν ("all your songs").

K. V begins the sentence with "and at that time one could see there."

L. *destruction*: PBC (cf. SlavZ) have καὶ οἰκιῶν διαφόρων καὶ ταμείων ἥξεις ("and shattering the different houses and rooms").

M. *value of gold* (PB cf. *Sermo de obit.*): V has "adornment (ὁ κόσμος) of gold."

N. These deportations and the capture of the sacred equipment from the

The Martyrdom of Daniel and the Three Youths

2 ¹And forty thousand men, women, and children were captured. Then the Assyrian (king) contrived to bind together a thousand men with an interwoven cord^A to one yoke^B and led^C the forty thousand out of their own city. ²Among the multitude of the captives, he set the three kindred Youths.^D In such a way, those (captives) who were ahead were dragged through uneven and impassable places with the horse's bridles like donkeys and mules, while those who were behind, were violently beaten to make them hurry up. ³For the king^E issued a command to lead them to their punishment^F all along the way barefoot.^G Then, when one of them got caught on the thorn and struggled to tear the thorn up from his foot, the thousands had to wait for the one. ⁴This was because they all were bound together as one, as the prophet^H predicted, saying, "*I was turned to wretchedness when a thorn was stuck in me.*"

Marginal references: 2 Kgs 24:16; 25:11; Jer 52:15 | LXX Ps 31:4

---

temple could happen in the period between 597–587 BCE; see DiTommaso, *Book of Daniel*, 39n3.

A. *with an interwoven cord* (cf. *Sermo de obit.*, SlavZ): lacking in V. *Pan. 3 Child.* 91–92 also reports about the nobles of Jerusalem being led to Babylon in chains.

B. *to one yoke*: lacking in PBC.

C. *and led*: V has "and in this manner forced."

D. The story about thousands of Judean captives who were led barefoot to Babylon, among whom were Daniel and the Three Youths, is present in abridged form in *Men*.

E. *the king*: lacking in PBC (cf. *Sermo de obit.*) but included here for clarity.

F. *to their punishment*: C has "for greater punishment."

G. Similar details about the Jews' sorrowful journey to Babylon are found in *Jer. Apocr.* 30. It is said that the Hebrews were led to Babylon for a month. During this time their sandals wore out and fell off along the way.

H. V adds "David" (cf. SlavZ).

The Heroic Deeds and the Contest

⁵Thus, having been beaten and walking on foot,^A they arrived in Babylon, which is on the third river.^B There [the instruments]^C were hung on trees and the Assyrians pressed hard saying, "Sing us a psalm in the same way you did in your land!" ⁶Then, the three kindred Youths stood up and said, "It is impossible to speak the words of God before unclean lips."^D Then, until the ninth hour that day they were humbled by the rod-bearers. The blameless^E Youths said, "We will praise the Lord^F in secret."

LXX Ps 136:1–4

⁷After that, about the third hour of night,^G the humanity-loving and forgiving God recalled the covenant with his servant^H Abraham and, considering^I the righteous ones, sent them healing angels. ⁸He restored his people unharmed from all malicious design and, having turned aside the heart of (their) enemies, he turned them sympathetically to them. ⁹After that, the king of Babylon saw a dream, which was hard to interpret, and wonderful signs.^J Learning the meaning of the dream^K from Daniel^L

A. *walking on foot*: πεζοποροῦντες from PB (cf. πεζοὶ ὁδοιπορήσαντες in *Sermo de obit.* and *Men.*). VC have περιζωπυροῦντες (inflamed). V adds "for forty days" (absent in PBC and SlavZ).

B. *on the third river*: lit. "of the third river." Babylon was situated between the Euphrates and Tigris Rivers. In addition, there was a system of canals used for irrigation as well as for transportation of food and goods. One such canal was the Chebar canal near Nippur (cf. Ezek 1:1). It is difficult to locate the exact place of "the third river," but the area near Chebar was used as a resettlement for various groups of deported nations, including Judeans; see Allen, *Psalms 101–150*, 307. According to 1 Bar. 1:4 the Jews lived in Babylon by the river Sud (Σουδ).

C. *the instruments*: the text does not specify what was hung up. *Sermo de obit.* implies that it was the captives who were hung upon the trees (but a full quotation of LXX Ps 136:2 follows).

D. *lips*: lacking in PBC. The story about the Jews forced by the Babylonians to sing psalms is found in *Jer. Apocr.* 31, 33, but without mention of the Three Youths.

E. V adds "and noble" (lacking in PBC and SlavZ).

F. V adds "*our God*" (lacking in PBC and SlavZ).

G. *of night*: lacking in PB.

H. *his servant*: lacking in PBC.

I. *considering*: SlavZ has "at the entreaty of."

J. *and wonderful signs* (PBC; cf. *Sermo de obit.*): lacking in V and SlavZ.

K. *learning . . . dream*: PBC have "the meanings of the king's dreams."

L. V has "the wise Daniel."

> and the holy Youths, he appointed them to be the rulers of the whole country.

Dan 2

3 ¹Three kingdoms had changed (in Babylon) since the resettlement of the Hebrews, but their mind did not change nor did they join in their faithlessness,^A nor participate in profanities.^B ²The thrice-happy, blessed, and holy^C Youths, accompanied by their good mentor Daniel,^D smashed the sixty-cubit profane image and killed the sixty-cubit dragon, which was regarded^E by them as a god.^F ³These writings^G of the holy ones were found written on crystal plates. For this reason, I thought it necessary to tell you their^H extraordinary and completely unknown story.

⁴After they smashed the statues of the profane gods^I by the power^J of the holy men, at the devil's advice of twisted malice, the furnace against the holy Youths was kindled.^K However, our Master, the Lord and God of all,^L sent his archangel Michael to them.^M After they were thrown to the furnace, the angel^N of God, stood

Ep Jer 3–5

Dan 3:1

Bel 3, 23–27

Dan 3:8–23

A. *their faithlessness* (PBC SlavZ): V has "their lawlessness and faithless decrees."

B. *profanities* (PBC; cf. *Sermo de obit.*): V has "participate with them profanely" (αὐτοῖς ματαίως).

C. *thrice-happy, blessed, and holy*: PBC have "three holy" (cf. SlavZ).

D. *Daniel*: lacking in PBC and SlavZ.

E. *regarded*: lacking in PBC.

F. V adds "and overturned Bel" (lacking in PBC and SlavZ).

G. *writings*: συγγράμματα. PBC have συντάγματα ("treatises").

H. *their*: PBC have "the."

I. *profane gods*: PBC have "profanities."

J. V adds "of God and" (lacking in PBC and SlavZ).

K. *at the devil's advice . . . was intended* PBC (cf. *Sermo de obit.* and SlavZ): V has "Daniel was thrown in the lions' den while the three holy Youths were thrown in the furnace of fire."

L. *our Master, the Lord and God of all*: PC have "God" (cf. SlavZ); B has "the humanity-loving, merciful God" (cf. *Sermo de obit.*).

M. The idea that it was the archangel Michael who was sent by God into the furnace is found in several Christian traditions—e.g., in Coptic Ps-Bachios of Maiuma, *On the Three Children*; Theodosius of Alexandria, *On the Archangel Michael*, as well as in some Coptic magic texts; see Sarrazin, "Three Holy Children."

N. *angel*: B has "the flame."

behind them[A] and cooled them down with water in the middle of the furnace.[B] All that day and night they were irrigated by dew, and rejoiced in the middle of the fire.[C] ⁵Therefore, the hair of their heads[D] was kept unsinged, and their faces were unchanged, and their feet were as if they were walking on drops (of dew). This was because the Spirit of the Almighty Lord was like a moist breeze whistling on them.[E]

Th. Dan 3:49–51
Dan 3:27

⁶And so the king cried out, saying, "Did we not throw the three men into the furnace? Behold, now I see four, and the appearance of the fourth is like a Son of God!"[F]

Th. Dan 3:91–92

⁷Then, Azarias turned[G] to him and said, "Tell me, O King, unlawful and doomed to violent death,[H] how can you, not knowing God, proclaim the Son of God? We have received every assault on his account, so that when he comes to us here in the flesh through the pure Virgin, as it is written, he may appoint us servants to be martyrs for his sake."[I]

Isa 7:14; 8:8
Matt 1:25; 2:1;
Luke 2:4–7

⁸Then, the king said, "And I see a holy one descending."

Th. Dan 4:13

⁹(Azarias) said, "Do you not understand that it is through the fear of God that you see the Holy of Holies?"[J]

A. *behind them*: lacking in P and SlavZ; C has "in the middle of the furnace."

B. *the angel of God . . . furnace*: B has "the fire of God."

C. V adds "glorifying God."

D. *the hair of their heads*: PBC have "their heads."

E. *the Spirit . . . on them*: PC have "the Spirit of the Lord was a moist breeze whistling on them"; B has "the Spirit of the Lord was changing the coals into dew."

F. *like a Son of God*: ὁμοία υἱῷ Θεοῦ (as in Th. Dan 3:92). OG Dan 3:92 reads ὁμοίωμα ἀγγέλου Θεοῦ and understands it as "a son of God" in relation to the angel. However, in the context of *Mart. Dan.* 3 this "Son of God" is clearly Jesus.

G. *turned*: lacking in PBC and SlavZ.

H. *unlawful and doomed to violent death*: ἀθέμιτε καὶ βιοθάνατε. B lacks βιοθάνατε. PC have ἀθέμιτε καὶ βωμολόχε ("unlawful and sacrilegious").

I. The author brings some Christian theological ideas into his paraphrasis of Th. Dan 3:91–93.

J. The vision of the angel of God in the furnace of fire in Dan 3 is probably fused here with that of the Lord's presence in the burning bush in Exod 3:2–14 or it is a reference to ἅγιον ἁγίων in Th. Dan 9:24.

The Martyrdom of Daniel and the Three Youths

Th. Dan
3:95–97

10Then Nebuchadnezzar, gripped by fear, understood, and believed.[A] He sent (a message) to those who are near and those who are far away and appointed the Youths to be rulers over Babylon. He fell asleep with faith in God.[B]

4 **1**Four months after his death, there arose a king of Persian lineage named Atticus.[C] He ruled the kingdom for thirty-four years and inquired about the Babylonian decrees.[D] He became aware of the virtue[E] and piety of the holy men Daniel and the Three Youths (and) ordered them[F] to be arrested.[G] **2**When they came and stood upon the judgment platform, he asked them,[H] "What is the wisdom of the Hebrews and whose parents do you happen to be descendants of?" Because of the guards around the throne all of those present were shuddering.[I] But the holy and thrice-blessed[J] Youths plucked up manly[K] courage and stood waving[L] their hand.

A. SlavZ inserts here (based on Th. Dan 3:93–94): "He ran up to the furnace, bowed down before them and said to them, 'Hananias, Azarias, and Misael, come out from the furnace! For I have realized that there is no other god who could have done this, who has turned the furnace cold.' And he added, 'Anybody who utters blasphemy against the living God, shall be destroyed!'"

B. C comes to an end here.

C. *Atticus*: Ἀττικός. The first story about Daniel and the Three Youths in UkS (fols. 105–109) does not contain the account of the martyrdom of Daniel and the Three Youths. However, it says that Atticus set up the Satanic idol, but Daniel expelled Satan from that idol and destroyed the pagan priests who served it (cf. the story of Bel and the Dragon).

D. *decrees*: δόγματα. PB have προστάγματα ("commandments").

E. *virtue*: lacking in PB (cf. *Sermo de obit.*).

F. *them* (cf. *Sermo de obit.*): lacking in VC.

G. In *Men. Basil II* this is briefly explained as that the king "found that these Three Holy Youths believed in God."

H. *when they came . . . asked them*: PB have "he stood on the judgment platform, inquiring."

I. *because . . . shuddering* (cf. *Sermo de obit.* and SlavZ): lacking in V.

J. *and thrice-blessed*: lacking in PB.

K. *manly*: lacking in PB.

L. *waving* (PB): V has "holding"; SlavZ "waving hands in the air." The sense here is a sign of refusal.

³Then, Misael began to give^A answer to the king and told him, "I am the youngest among the Youths like me but they do not want to talk with you because they consider you an abomination. I am compelled first of all to say this concerning you. ⁴For so far I myself respond to the foolishness of the insensibility of your desire, because you are worse than crawling^B and poisonous animals, which bring up fire through their lips and then extinguish it. ⁵For calling those^C a god, you pour bloody food^D over the image of a dog or a wolf. ⁶So, it is given to your kind and to your tribe to prosper on earth for the purpose of cursed hypocrisy,^E as did Magedon,^F your father, who because of illusory wealth,

---

A. *to give*: reading ἀπονέμειν for ἐπομένην (Istrin suggests ἀπομένειν).

B. *crawling*: B has "creeping."

C. *those*: PB have "this," which may relate to fire (πῦρ) in the previous sentence: "calling this [fire] god." See *Sermo de obit.*: "because the fire kindled through our lips you call god."

D. *bloody food*: αἱμοβόρων.

E. *hypocrisy*: SlavZ has "the condemnation."

F. *Magedon*: Μαγεδῶν. This name is not associated with any historical Persian ruler. Misael states that this king decided to marry because of the wealth of certain women, but this information does not help to identify him. In any case, the context implies its negative meaning. In the LXX (Josh 12:22; Judg 1:27; 2 Chr 35:22), Μαγεδῶν relates to the valley of Megiddo. Cf. also Ἁρμαγεδών in Rev 16:16 which can mean the hill of Megiddo. Μαγεδῶν may relate to Greek μάγος, which is of Persian origin. In some contexts, it is used for Persian priests and magicians (cf. Matt 2:1). It also can relate to μαγουδαῖος or μαγουσαῖος. The former is found in John of Damascus, *Epistula ad Theophilum imperatorem de sacris imaginibus* 11 (*PG* 95:360A). He describes them as magicians (φαρμακοί), enchanters (ἐπαοιδοί), and astrologists (γαζαρηνοί). Μαγουδαῖος can be a conflation of μάγος and Ἰουδαῖος and mean Jewish magician; Lampe, *Greek Patristic Lexicon*, 819. De Jong (*Traditions of the Magi*, 404n58), however, argues that this word is "a mistake for Μαγουσαῖος, since it is willfully paralleled to the Magi of Matt 2, but adding a pejorative meaning." Apart from use as a synonym of μάγοι as Persian priests and more generally Zoroastrians (as in Coptic Manichaean texts; see de Jong, *Traditions of the Magi*, 405nn63–64), Μαγουσαῖοι is used for adepts of a Persian esoteric sect, "widespread in eastern provinces, holding esoteric doctrines, practicing vegetarianism, worshipping heavenly bodies, and accused of incestuous marriages" (Lampe, *Greek Patristic Lexicon*, 819). This word occurs in Greek and Latin Christian texts (see, e.g., Ps.-Clem., *Rec.* 20.20–21; Basil the Great, *Ep.* 258.4; Eusebius of Caesarea, *Praep. ev.* 6.10.16.4, 6.10.38.3; Epiphanius of Salamis, *Ancor.* 113.2.3; *Pan.* 3.512.18; 3.512.23; Leontius of Byzantium, *Contra Nestorianos* 3.1376.32; 3.1384.40; Georgius Hamartolus, *Chronicon*

The Martyrdom of Daniel and the Three Youths

being in companionship with the Syrians,[A] attached himself to a marital partnership. [7]For which reason, on the instigation of the unclean water spirit, you have learned to kill and consume the offspring of cows and bulls by fire; you regard this unlawful shameless act as a sacrifice. Mixing their blood with dough, you do not realize that you are eating their own flesh, and therefore you are also called Manichaeans.[B]

[8]"Finally, I will shout about us: we are children of pious rulers, father Hezekiah and mother Kallegonia,[C] who dared to say

---

breve 110:141), as well as in Coptic Manichaean texts. Another strand of interpretation of Magedon is found in the Church Slavonic tradition. See the commentary on SlavZ 4:6 below.

A. *Syrians*: the text has the unusual form συρίναις. *Men.* has *sürẹnynẹmi* ("the Syrians"). The Greek author/editor/scribe could have confused the spelling of συρίαι with συρίναι. According to Basil the Great, Magusaeans practiced not only incestuous marriages (γάμοις ἐπιμαίνονται παρανόμοις; this may refer to Magedon's marriage with the Syrians), but also consider fire to be a god (τὸ πῦρ ἡγοῦνται Θεὸν) (*Ep.* 258.4; cf. *Mart. Dan.* 4:4–5). It is also interesting that the earliest reference to Μαγουσαῖοι is found in the Syrian author Bardaisan of Edessa, *Bk. Laws* (*mgūshā*; Drijvers, *Book of the Laws*, 44, 54; Lund, *Book of the Laws*, 162). This indicates the presence of Zoroastrianism in Syria (de Jong, *Traditions of the Magi*, 406). On the other hand, since B has σειρίσι, συρίναις can be a confused reading of σειρῇσι (Σειρῆνες/Συρίνες; "Sirens" or "deceitful women"), which is how SlavZ 4:6 renders the term.

B. Despite all similarities with Magusaeans, whoever they would have been, Atticus and his father Magedon are identified as Manichaeans, who also have Persian roots. However, the characteristics of Manichaeans given here hardly correspond to what is known about the historical adepts of this religious group. Moreover, the existence of the Manichaeans in Persia at the time of Daniel and the Three Youths is an obvious anachronism. Therefore, we have here a mixture of popular prejudices of several religious groups.

C. *Kallegonia*: Καλληγόνη. In contrast to Hezekiah, who is known from the biblical account, Kallegonia remains an enigmatic figure. Probably, her name refers to her personality and means simply "a good parent/mother." SlavR renders it as *dobrorodnyẹ* ("noble"). According to the biblical account of Hezekiah, his wife's name was Hephzibah. She gave birth to Hezekiah's son Manasseh (2 Kgs 21:1). The Bible does not mention the Three Youths as Hezekiah's children. Though, in Dan 1:3 they are mentioned among the young men of the royal family and of noble families. According to the Ethiopic tradition, the Three Youths were the sons of Joachim, the king of Judah, and Daniel was a son of their sister (Budge, *Book of the Saints*, 3:726). In *Syn. Alex.*, Daniel was from Joachim's (*Younâkhir*) family (*PO* 16:247). The Coptic *Pan. 3 Child.* 70 (De Vis, *Homélies Coptes*, 60) conveys the same idea. According to this account, Joachim had four sons (Jechonias, Hannaias, Azarias, and

The Heroic Deeds and the Contest

to God, '*I have done the things that are pleasing in your sight, and walked before you in truth*,' who received from God the addition of fifteen more years,[A] and who had forgiven the tribute of the farmers.[B] **9**This one foretold, saying to us that in due time the Word of God will come in the form of a human being, who will open Hades and illuminate the darkness.[C] (This Word) we also saw in a shadow manner before that time, when we trampled the fire under the king who ruled before you,[D] who was, however, deemed worthy of salvation. **10**But what will be with you on the day of visitation? At that time you will suffer. But now, what you want to do against us,[E] do it quickly, for we willingly accept death for the sake of God."

LXX 4 Kgdms 20:3, 6; LXX Isa 38:3, 5

Wis 3:7
John 13:27

5 ¹Angered at this answer, the king consulted with his advisers and ordered the beheading of Misael. Having run up and stretched out his cloak, Azarias received his[F] head and cried. ²But Atticus also ordered the beheading of Azarias. Then, Hananias, having run up, enfolded both[G] heads[H] in his cloak and said, "We will go together to our Lord and Savior of the world." ³After that, bowing his[I] neck, he also was beheaded. And Daniel, hav-

---

Misael) and one daughter, Mariam (cf. Dan 1:6). She became the mother of Daniel. His father, whose name in this story is Simeon, was a ruler of the tribe of Judah and appointed chiefs over the entire service of the kings of Judah.

A. *addition of fifteen more years*: an allusion to the biblical story of Hezekiah's recovery after his prayer to the Lord: he was granted fifteen more years of life (2 Kgs 20:1–11; Isa 38; 2 Chr 32:24–26).

B. *forgiven . . . farmers*: this probably refers to Hezekiah's religious reforms (2 Kgs 18:1–8; 2 Chr 29–31) and his wealth after the defeat of the Assyrians (2 Chr 32:27–30) that could have some impact on farmers. However, in *Sermo de obit.* 4:9 it is described as an act of mercy.

C. *Hades . . . darkness*: (PB; cf. SlavZ and *Sermo de obit.*). V has "world . . . world."

D. *we also saw . . . darkness*: such a statement can be based on the mention of "the son of God" in Th. Dan 3:92 and relate to the earlier episode of this story (*Mart. Dan.* 3:7).

E. *what you want to do against us*: lacking in PB.

F. V adds "venerable and holy."

G. V adds "venerable and holy."

H. *heads*: lacking in P.

I. V adds "venerable" (lacking in PB and SlavZ).

ing stretched out his robe on the ground, received the[A] heads of the three, bowed his head, and was also beheaded.[B]

⁴All Israel mourned for them with great weeping. Then they collected the remains[C] of the saints and, having enlisted skilled silversmiths, made coffins and placed the departed in them,[D] engraving on each chest the names of those who were laid there.[E] Suddenly, their heads joined each to its own body.[F] ⁵Since the king wanted to burn their remains, the angels took them at night and brought them to Mount Gebal to hide them.[G] Immediately,

A. V adds "holy" (lacking in PB and SlavZ).

B. V adds "on 17 December" (lacking in PB and SlavZ, but see *Sermo de obit.* 5:8). This is the day (the week before the feast of Nativity) of the Youths' liturgical commemoration in the Byzantine tradition. The description of the martyrdom is very brief. In most details it corresponds to what is written in *Syn. Cp.* 319 (see appendix B).

C. *remains*: PB have "bodies." Cf. *tĕlesa* in *Men*.

D. *placed the departed in them*: lacking in PB.

E. PB add "they were put into the coffins."

F. In UkS 3:12, it is the archangel Michael who reunites their bodies and heads. Probably this reading alludes to Jude 1:9, where Michael is said to have taken care of the body of Moses and disputed about it with the devil. Similarly, in Targum Pseudo-Jonathan on Deut 34:6, Michael and Gabriel (together with Metatron and three other ministering angels) prepare Moses' burial and arrange a golden couch for him. See also the story about the archangel Michael with Gabriel, Uriel, and Rafael who take care of Adam's and Abel's bodies and bury them in paradise (LAE 40). The motif of decapitated heads reattaching themselves to bodies is most well-known in a story incorporated into the *Epistle of Pseudo-Dionysius the Areopagite to Timothy* where the head of the apostle Paul joins his body after his execution (9:11–19). See the discussion in Eastman, "Epistle," 469.

G. *Gebal*: *Syn. Cp.* 319 also calls this mountain Gebal. The mountain עֵיבָל (*'ēbāl*) is located in Samaria (Deut 27:4; Josh 8:30, 33). From this mountain the curses for Israel were proclaimed (Deut 11:29; 27:13; Josh 8:32–35). Moreover, some large stones with the words of the Law were set up there (Deut 27:2–4) and the first altar to the Lord that Joshua built after crossing the river Jordan was on this mountain. In addition, this mountain also appears in *Acts Andr. Phlm.* 7:14–26, where Andrew resuscitates a dismembered child by reciting a prayer that mentions a miracle performed by Jesus on Mount Ebal. Jesus performed this miracle in a way similar to how Joshua (who is probably identified with Jesus in this text) gathered his altar from scattered grains of sand. In the LXX עֵיבָל (*'ēbāl*) is rendered as Γαιβαλ. It was common for the LXX translators to transliterate ע (ʿ) as γ (cf. the rendering of עַזָּה [*'azzâ*] as Γάζα in, for example, Gen 10:19; Deut 2:23; Josh 10:41; 11:22). In contrast to Γαιβαλ, Γεβαλ in the LXX is a territory to the southeast of the Dead Sea (LXX Ps 82:8; cf. Hebrew גְּבָל [*gĕbāl*]). In the Hebrew Bible, גְּבָל

The Heroic Deeds and the Contest

the rock split apart[A] and hid the remains.[B] After the return of the children of Israel and the restoration of Jerusalem, the remains of the holy ones were in Babylon[C] until the time of the coming of the Master in the flesh.[D]

⁶When the Jews set up the Cross against our Lord Jesus Christ, when the foundations of the ground trembled and were shaken from seeing God being given over to the grave, when heaven trembled, rocks were broken in pieces, the tops of mountains trembled, when all of Hades was illuminated, *many bodies of the saints who had fallen asleep were raised and having entered*

(*gĕbāl*) is also another name for the city Byblos (cf. Ezek 27:9). There is also a reference to Γεβαλ in T. Levi 6:1, which is the place located near Mount Aspis (Ἀσπίς) to the right of Abila (Ἀβιλά). However, its location is uncertain. Therefore, it is most probable that in *Mart. Dan.*, Gebal relates to the biblical mountain Ebal. The change of αι to ε, as it seen in some other cases in this text, could be due to the phonetic features of the Byzantine spelling. It is also interesting that in *Men.* and SlavZ 5:5 this mountain is *Egevalŭ* while in SlavR it is *Gevalĭ*. So bringing the bodies of Daniel and the Three Youths to Ebal may represent the idea that while Jews were still in exile in Babylon, these righteous ones were brought back to Israel to be hidden on the mountain where Israel's first sacrifice was offered in the promised land.

A. *apart*: lit. "in itself." B has "in the earth."

B. V adds "of the holy ones" (lacking in PB and SlavZ).

C. This seems to contradict what is said above about the location of the remnants of Daniel and the Three Youths in Gebal. According to *Syn. Cp.* 319, "they were placed there under the rock for 400 years" until the resurrection of Christ. In the Armenian tradition, their location and how long they are on the mountain is more complicated. *Arm. Syn.*[2] also indicates Mount Gebal. However, in *Arm.*, Daniel and the Three Youths were first buried in the palace of Nebuchadnezzar but then somehow appeared to a pious Persian prince of Babylon named Mazlut'a (cf. *Arm. Syn.*[4]) and were reburied in the region of Kołt'n in the Armenian province of Vaspurakan. According to *Arm. Syn.*[2], *Arm. Syn.*[4], and *Arm.*, their first burial was in Babylon. *Alexandria*[2] and *Alexandria*[4] (2.17) also localize it in Babylon. Moreover, the editors of *Alexandria*[2] and *Alexandria*[4] joined together the legend of their peaceful departure and the legend of their martyrdom; see Istrin, *Alexandria*, 185. The Coptic and Ethiopic traditions report an unsuccessful attempt to bring the bodies of the Three Youths from Babylon to Alexandria, where the archbishop Theophilus (late 4th cent. CE) built a church dedicated to the Three Youths (*Syn. Alex.* [PO 16:353–54]; Budge, *Book of the Saints*, 3:173–74). According to *Vit. Mac. Rom.* (ed. Vassiliev 137), the relics of the Three Youths were deposited in Ctesiphon, an ancient city located on the eastern bank of the Tigris.

D. *in the flesh*: likely a reference to the incarnation of Christ. SlavR adds that they were there until the Crucifixion.

The Martyrdom of Daniel and the Three Youths

Matt 27:51–53   *the holy city appeared to many.*[A] ⁷Among whom were Abel and Noah, Abraham, Isaac and Jacob, Joseph, Isaiah, Jeremiah, and Baruch, John the Forerunner of Christ, and Hezekiah with his spouse. Then their own three kindred Youths Hananias, Azarias, and Misael, and their mentor and the wise Daniel were raised,[B] ⁸and, in a word, also a great multitude of others, more than 500, from the great number of those whom the Master had chosen, and who went[C] to paradise. Others he commanded to fall asleep until his second coming. ⁹That is why Paul says, *"He appeared to more than five hundred brothers and sisters at one time, most of*

1 Cor 15:6   *whom are still alive, though some have died."* Those whom he sent to paradise remain there until now, but those whom he sent to fall asleep are asleep until his second coming.[D]

     A. B adds "and I said."

     B. Both *Mart. Dan.* and *Sermo de obit.* give a list of the names of those saints who were resurrected, but the list in *Mart. Dan* (see also SlavZ) is more extensive. According to some Georgian witnesses of the Sinaitic Palestino-Georgian calendar (10th cent. CE) the risen saints who appeared in the holy city together with Adam were commemorated on the Wednesday of the fourth week after Easter; see Garitte, *Calendrier*, 429–30. The idea of the resurrection of Daniel and the Three Youths may have come as an allusion to Dan 12:2–3, 13: "Many of those who sleep in the dust of the earth shall awake, some to everlasting life, and some to shame and everlasting contempt. Those who are wise shall shine like the brightness of the sky, and those who lead many to righteousness, like the stars forever and ever . . . But you, go your way, and rest; you shall rise for your reward at the end of the days." It is interesting that in *Pan. 3 Child.*, as in many other accounts of these righteous ones, they die but are not martyred. However, the Son of God promises to the Three Youths that in his coming (i.e., the Parousia) their bodies will shine like the sun (87). Further, according to this account, Daniel and the Three Youths peacefully died in Babylon: the Three Youths died on 10 Pashons (the ninth month of the Coptic calendar; 86–88) and were buried in ivory tombs (Nebuchadnezzar was later buried between them in a golden bed; 89), while Daniel lived a long life during the reign of Nebuchadnezzar, Baltasar, Cyrus, Darius, and Abdiakis (Cambyses?), and died on 21 Choiak (the fourth month of the Coptic calendar) and was buried together with the kings of Judah (97, 99). At the same time, this text explicitly mentions Matt 27:51–53, but without any reference to Daniel and the Three Youths (110).

     C. *went*: PB have "sent."

     D. *until his second coming*: instead, PB have γένονε δὲ ταῦτα διὰ τὴν πρᾶξιν τῆς ἀναστασίας ("this came about as a result of the resurrection"; cf. SlavZ). Paul's words in 1 Cor 15:6 about the five hundred brethren to whom the resurrected Jesus appeared are interpreted in this story as five

The Heroic Deeds and the Contest

¹⁰Therefore, having struggled in the same way, the three holy and blameless Youths were preserved[A] under the rock for 440 years.[B] And they were brought back to their own place,[C] by the grace and love for humanity of our Lord Jesus Christ, to him be glory and power now and always and forever. Amen.

---

hundred saints who were resurrected together with Jesus. Some of them were commanded to go to paradise and remain there, while others had to die again until the second coming of the Lord. According to *Sermo de obit.* 4:13, among the many who were to go to paradise were the Three Youths, Daniel, and Hezekiah.

A. *the three holy and blameless Youths were preserved* (PB and SlavZ): V has "the thrice-blessed and thrice-happy blameless Youths, earlier preserved by the All-holy and consubstantial Trinity."

B. *440 years*: four hundred years in *Syn. Cp.* 319 and Dmitry of Rostov, *Lives of the Saints* 128; seven hundred years in *Arm. Syn.*².

C. *they were brought back to their own place*: in an effort to harmonize with Matt 27:53, V prefaces this statement with "together with the prophet Daniel, they were raised at the holy resurrection of Christ" (lacking in PB and SlavZ). *Syn. Cp.* 319 directly states that Daniel and the Three Youths soon died again: "At the time of the resurrection of our Lord Jesus Christ, they were also raised together with him and passed away again." In this interpretation, this was not the bodily resurrection to eternal life but the temporary restoration of physical life. In *Mart. Dan., Sermo de obit.*, SlavZ, and UkS the idea is more complicated. After the resurrection, Daniel and the Three Youths go to paradise, but it is not clear whether they are taken there in corporeal or incorporeal form and whether it is a place reserved for the righteous before their future resurrection or their final blessed destination.

The Sermon on the Demise of the Three Holy Youths and the All-Wise Daniel by Our Holy Father Cyril, Archbishop of Alexandria

1 ¹The occasion of times^A has come, beloved ones, to commemorate the good martyrs. For this memory imitates the festal assembly^B of the heavenly ranks for the intercession and salvation of our souls. Therefore, as much as you know God—but more so, Gal 4:9 you are known by him^C—today then, lend me your ears, so that you can be deemed worthy of the price of the aforementioned^D martyrs. ²For those who never saw the incarnation of Christ and the death of the Immortal One and the resurrection from the dead should praise and marvel at those who became his confessors and witnesses even before [his] coming in flesh. ³About them the providence of the undefiled Trinity teaches^E through the prophecy that has just been read for the sake of the kingly and kindred^F Youths Hannaias, Azarias, and Misael, and the prophet Daniel.^G ⁴About their way of life and citizenship and correspond-

---

A. *of times*: D has "in time."

B. *imitates the festal assembly*: lacking in D.

C. *but more so, you are known by him*: added from D (cf. *Mart. Dan.*; UkS).

D. *aforementioned*: D has "impurely sacrificed."

E. *teaches*: lacking in R.

F. *kindred*: ὁμόφυλος (cf. ὁμόγονος in *Mart. Dan.*).

G. *and the prophet Daniel* (cf. *Mart. Dan.* 1:4): lacking in R.

ing knowledge, their alliance^A and death I would like to narrate to the church of God; about how, having behaved in an upright manner, the Youths of the good branch died.^B

⁵Jerusalem, Jerusalem, what do I set before you? How shall I call to mind your acts and way of life? ⁶Not once nor twice, but three and four times it was commanded through the prophet Isaiah,^C "*Wash yourselves, become clean*" (and) "*learn to do good,*^D *rescue the one who is wronged. O city Jerusalem, in you righteousness lodged and murderers stand beside you.*" ⁷[God] warns through the prophet Micah saying, "*I will turn your hearts*^E *to mourning and your joy to lamentation. And I will deport you beyond* Babylon."^F

⁸Because [Jerusalem] did not incline to obedience,^G he prepares the king of Assyria in remembrance of the treasure of Hezekiah, in order to fulfill the word of the prophet, "*they shall take also some of your children whom you have begotten and shall make them eunuchs*^H *in the house*^I *of the king of the Babylonians.*" ⁹Therefore, he will stand against you seventy thousand chosen troops of the chief men^J skilled in waging war, furious swift horses, on which were mounted heavily armed young archers equipped with armor, who also are able to^K successfully throw out sharp^L javelins and not miss. ¹⁰Then the king attacked the city at the third watch of the night. There was a feast with a torchlit procession, with a drunken party and stomping, dances, cymbals,

LXX Isa 1:16–17, 21

Amos 5:27; 8:10

2 Kgs 18:13–16; Isa 36:1
LXX Isa 39:7; LXX 4 Kgdms 20:18

2 Kgs 25:1; Hab 1:6–10; Dan 1:1

    A. *alliance*: συμμαχία.

    B. *good branch*: καλλίκλαδοι (cf. Constantinus Manasses, *Syn. Hist.* 5197, 6355). D has καλλοικέλαδοι; M has καλοὶ κλάδοι ("good branches").

    C. *but three . . . Isaiah*: in *Mart. Dan.* it is told four times through David in LXX Ps 88:31.

    D. D adds: "seek judgment" (as in LXX Isa 16:17).

    E. *hearts*: D has "anger."

    F. On this composite quotation, see the note to *Mart. Dan.* 1:7.

    G. *because . . . obedience*: ὥς οὖν οὐκ ἐπένευσεν τῇ ἀκοῇ (D; cf. *Mart. Dan.*), ὅσον νῦν ἐπένευσεν τῇ ἀκοῇ (R). Istrin emends ἀκοῇ to ὑπακοῇ.

    H. *eunuchs*: σπάδονας. D has σπονδάς ("libation").

    I. *the house*: lacking in R.

    J. *chief men*: ἄνδρας δυνάστας. Istrin has δονάστας.

    K. *are able to*: R has "from behind."

    L. *sharp*: reading τῶν ἀκίδων for τῶν ἀδίκων. D has τῶν κείδων.

The Martyrdom of Daniel and the Three Youths

percussion and buzzing lyres, and a monstrous image of those who danced.^A ^11^Neither the nobles nor the free ones were away from the city, but the whole city of the different classes of people was gathered, equally engaged in the drunken bout. ^12^But Jeremiah was crying saying, "*How long until you will be quiet, O God?*" ^13^The prophet Baruch, unable to bear their lawless deed, locked himself in the chasm. For three days^B the prophet Abimelech stayed outside of the city^C sleeping in order not to see the misfortune that occurred.

^14^When the king of the Babylonians suddenly appeared, a buzzing^D trumpet echoed greatly in seven ranks like a violent thunder and iron-footed mechanical wheels, spinning around, crushed the walls, leveling them down. ^15^The pounding of chariots and barbarous and the mad chaos of warriors, quivers clashed together and furious horses whinnying with a barbarous noise, gnashed loudly.^E ^16^Trumpets cried out like thunder calling to both heaven and earth, so that the drunken party was immediately hidden away, the dance disappeared, and cymbals were removed^F—according to the prophet saying, "*to change their feasts into mourning and their joy into lamentation*"—and then instead of cymbals (there was) grieving, instead of a torch mist and darkness, instead of light fear and trembling. (There was) in that place collapsed walls, the plundering of households,^G burning and boiling up, and a confusion of corpses at the sides of the temple. ^17^All the equipment of the order^H for the Lord's liturgy

References (margin): LXX Jer 29:6; MT Jer 47:6; 4 Bar. 4:7–12; 4 Bar. 3:15–16; 5:1–2; Josh 6:16; 2 Kgs 25:10; Jer 52:14; LXX Amos 8:10; Jer 52:13

A. *a monstrous image . . . danced*: φασματικὸς τύπος τῶν ὀρχουμένων. Cf. κτύπος τῶν ὀρχουμένων ("the stomping of those who were dancing") in *Mart. Dan.*; κτύπος could be a corruption of τύπος or vice versa.

B. In 4 Bar. 3:15–16 Abimelech went outside of Jerusalem in the early morning right before the Babylonians attacked the city. He spent there not three days but sixty-six years.

C. *outside of the city*: lit. ἐν ἀγρῷ ("in a field").

D. *buzzing* (cf. *Mart. Dan.*): R has ἐκκλινούσης ("distorting"?).

E. *pounding . . . loudly*: the sentence has difficulties. See the note to the parallel material in *Mart. Dan.*

F. *and cymbals were removed*: lacking in D. Reading ῥίπτεσθαι here for ῥύπτεσθαι ("washed").

G. *households*: οἰκείων. D has σκύλων ("of spoils").

H. *of the order*: lacking in D.

The Sermon on the Demise of the Three Holy Youths

and God's mystery,^A which was not a countless value of silver, were plundered. All these things were brought out of Jerusalem by the captive sons of Israel.^B

2 ^1When forty thousand of men, women, and children were captured, the Assyrian [king] then contrived to line the forty thousand up with a cord to one yoke and brought them out from the holy city. Among these (forty) thousand were set three kindred^C Youths, who were bound with fetters.^D ^2And in such a way [the king] commanded that those bound with cords who were ahead to be led^E through uneven and inaccessible places like driven donkeys, while those who were behind to be violently beaten to make them hurry up, because they were led to the punishment barefoot.^F ^3When one of them got caught on the thorn and, being unceasingly in pain, struggled to tear the thorn up from his foot, he broke up the line of the whole group, which had to wait for the one, because the thousands^G had to be always in one chain. ^4According to the singing of the prophet, "*I was turned to wretchedness when a thorn was stuck in me.*" And again,^H "*Do not be like horse and mule, who have no understanding.*" For if they bore God's love of humanity, they would not be led to Babylon like a mule being pierced with a spear.^I

^5Thus, being vigorously prodded while walking on foot for forty days, they were brought to Babylon near the river Stoigion.^J

Marginal references: 2 Kgs 24:10—25:17; 2 Chr 36:17–20; Jer 52:13–23; Dan 1:2 · 2 Kgs 24:16; 25:11; Jer 52:15 · LXX Ps 31:4 · LXX Ps 31:9

    A. *mystery*: μυσταγωγίας. In the early church μυσταγωγία is an introduction to the Christian doctrines and mysteries.

    B. *by the captive sons of Israel*: R simply has "the captives."

    C. *kindred*: ὁμογόνους (cf. *Mart. Dan.*); R has μόνους ("only").

    D. *bound with fetters*: lacking in R.

    E. *to be led*: lacking in R.

    F. *barefoot* (ἀνυπόδητοι) (cf. *Mart. Dan.*): R renders it as δίχα πῶν ὑποδημάτων ("in two ... sandals").

    G. *thousands*: D has "forty thousand."

    H. *according to ... and again* (cf. *Mart. Dan.*): R has "about them the prophet cried out, saying."

    I. R adds "and again, 'when a thorn was stuck in me.'"

    J. *river Stoigion*: the location of this river is unclear. In D it is τοῦ ἁγίου ποταμοῦ ("the holy river"). *Mart. Dan.* has "the third river." SlavR renders it as "Geon." In UkS 1:8 it is called "Asidon."

The Martyrdom of Daniel and the Three Youths

LXX Ps 136:1–4 — There having been hung upon the brunches of the willow and continuously beaten, they were compelled by the foreigners saying, "Sing us a psalm, the same way[A] you did in your land." As the prophet, foreseeing, cried out, *"on the willows in its midst we* LXX Ps 136:2 — *hung our instruments."* ⁶Then, the three blameless Youths stood up and raised their voice, saying, "It is impossible to speak the words of God on unclean land." They were humbled by the rod-bearers until the ninth hour. The holy Youths, weeping, recited [psalms] to themselves, and commending to the legion, "We will praise God secretly, because God has delivered us to the hands of the lawless ones who refused to listen to his commandments."

⁷After that, about the tenth hour of the day, the humanity-loving and forgiving God recalled the covenant of the fathers and considered the weariness[B] of the people, because he is quick in mercy. ⁸He restored his people unharmed from all lawless design and, having turned aside the hearts of (their) enemies,[C] he made them sympathetic. ⁹After that, when the dreams which were hard to interpret and the signs and wonders were explained by Daniel and the Holy Youths, the king of Babylon appointed them to be the rulers of the satraps over that whole country, so that their Dan 2 — captive kinsmen could be instructed in proper knowledge.[D]

3 ¹Now three kingdoms had changed in Babylon since the resettlement of the Hebrews, but the people did not participate Ep Jer 3–5 — in profanities. ²The holy Youths, accompanied by their mentor Dan 3:1 — Daniel, smashed the sixty-cubit profane image and struck down Bel 3, 23–27 — the great dragon. ³Whoever is the most devoted, lend me your[E] ears: may no one, having turned to carelessness, run away from the covenant of the fathers.[F]

A. *the same way*: D has "as (you did)."

B. *considered the weariness*: ἀξιωθεὶς ἐν τῇ κακήσει. Cf. ἀξιωθεὶς παρὰ τῶν δικαίων in *Mart. Dan.* D has: μεαβληθεὶς ἐπὶ τῇ κακώσει ("stirred by the weariness").

C. *enemies* (cf. *Mart. Dan.*): R has "lawless."

D. *proper knowledge*: lacking in R.

E. *your* (cf. 1:1): lacking in R.

F. *the fathers*: D has "his fathers."

The Sermon on the Demise of the Three Holy Youths

⁴Today, the Divine Word says in the hidden books of Daniel that after smashing the profane statues by the goodwill of the gloriously triumphant martyrs,^A by the advice of twisted malice, the furnace against the Youths^B was kindled. However, the humanity-loving God without delay^C sent the archangel^D Michael and they spent all that day and night^E being irrigated by dew, lodging in the middle of the fire. ⁵Their hair was kept unsinged, their faces were unchanged, their sandals were collected from the fire like they were a drop of melting dew,^F because the wind of dew was whistling. So great was the fire pouring out that it was about forty-nine cubits, signifying the seven weeks of holy Lent.^G

⁶And so King Nebuchadnezzar cried out, saying, "Did we not throw the three men into the furnace? But now I see four walking in it,^H and the appearance of the fourth is like a Son of God!"^I

⁷Azarias said, "Tell me, O King, how you, not knowing God—more so, are not known by him^J—can proclaim the Son of God? For we endure every assault for on his account, so that when the Messiah comes, he who will be begotten according to the flesh in Bethlehem of Judea,^K he who appeared in the thornbush,^L by

Dan 3:8–23

Th. Dan 3:49–51
Dan 2:27

Th. Dan 3:47, 94

Th. Dan 3:92

Gal 4:9

Matt 1:25; 2:1; Luke 2:4–7
Exod 3:2–14

A. *martyrs*: D has "youths."

B. *the Youths*: D has "them."

C. *without delay*: lacking in D.

D. *archangel* (cf. *Mart. Dan.*): lacking in R.

E. *day and night*: from Istrin's emendation τὸ νυχθήμερον; the manuscripts have τὸν ἠχθήμενον.

F. *their sandals . . . dew*: D has "their sandals were like a drop of dew, indeed as if fire had not been found on their clothing."

G. The Great Lent in the Eastern Orthodox tradition begins seven weeks before Easter.

H. *but now I see four walking in it* (cf. *Mart. Dan.*): lacking in R.

I. *like a Son of God*: see the comment on *Mart. Dan.* 3:6.

J. *more so . . . by him*: cf. 1:1.

K. SlavR adds: "in the ark of the manger."

L. *he who appeared in the thornbush*: D has "from the girl who had not known man." R follows the christological interpretation of the appearance of the Lord in the burning bush in Exod 3:2–14 and connects this appearance with that of the son of God in the furnace of fire in Th. Dan 3:92. The idea that it was Christ who appeared before Moses in the burning bush is found already in Justin Martyr (*Dial.* 59.1; 127.4), then, in Irenaeus (*Epid.*

The Martyrdom of Daniel and the Three Youths

Isa 7:14; 8:8 means of our kinswoman according to what was predicted in the Law, as our blessed mother taught us,[A] then passing on, we will be among the martyrs brought to him."[B]

Th. Dan 4:13 ⁸Then the king said, "Do I see Ir and a holy one descending?"[C]

⁹Azarias said in response, still standing in the middle of the fire, "Do you not perceive this, uncomprehending king, that all agree that Ir is called the holy assistance?[D] Perceive, O King, that

Th. Dan 3:92 you saw the fourth who comes according to the flesh in due time."

46; *Haer.* 3.6.2; 4.10.1), Tertullian (*Prax.* 16.6), Clement of Alexandria (*Paed.* 2.8.75.1–2), Origen (*Comm. Cant.* 2.8.8; *Comm. Rom.* 10.8.5). See further references in Bucur, *Scripture Re-Envisioned*, 82–100. Athanasius of Alexandria also supported the christological interpretation of this episode. In Eastern iconography the Nativity and the Theophany in the burning bush are sometimes connected (Bucur, *Scripture Re-Envisioned*, 108–9). On the other hand, the virgin Mary was often associated with the burning bush from Exod 3:2–5 (e.g., Gregory of Nyssa, *Diem nat.* PG 46:1136B).

A. Azarias mentions the mother of the Three Youths, who is, as we will find out later in the story, named Kallegonia, the wife of King Hezekiah.

B. *then . . . to him*: D has "then he will gather us together from the fetters of Hades." This refers to the resurrection of Daniel and the Three Youths, which will be mentioned further.

C. *do I see . . . descending*: εἲρ καὶ ἅγιον θεωρῶ καταβῆναι. SlavR omits this reading. However, SlavU reads, "I see a cloud and a holy one." Here, the author switches to the vision from Dan 4:10–14. Ip is a transliteration of Aramaic עִיר (*ʿîr*) ("watcher"). The spelling of ιρ as εἲρ was common. Εἲρ was interpreted by some commentators as "storm" or "lighting" (Theodoridis, *Photii Patriarchae Lexicon*, 26; Latte and Cunningham, *Hesychii Alexandrini Lexicon*, 41) but also as "wakeful," "awaken" (ἄγρυπνος; Polychronius of Apamea, *Comm. Dan.* 4.23.2; Isidor of Pelusium, 2.177 *Theod. Presb.* 20; ἐγρηγορότα; Theodoret of Cyrus, *Interp. Dan.* PG 81:1360). Aquila and Symmachus render עִיר (*ʿîr*) as ἐγρήγορος ("wakeful one," "watcher"). This probably relates to the tradition about the Watchers as the angelic beings in early Jewish literature, especially in 1 En. 1–36, which is approximately contemporary with Dan 1–6 (Collins, *Commentary*, 224–25). In this case, the author of *Sermo de obit.* follows the interpretation of εἲρ as related to the Watchers (cf., e.g., 1 En. 1:5; 10:7; 12:3). Furthermore, Hippolytus of Rome regards εἲρ καὶ ἅγιος as an angel coming from heaven (*Comm. Dan.* 3.9.1; cf. OG Dan 4:13), but, on the other hand, he interprets ἅγιος as relating to the Word of God (3.9.6). Isidor of Pelusium regards εἲρ as archangel (οἱονεὶ ἀρχάγγελον; literary, "as if archangel") and a wakeful one (ἄγρυπνος), while ἅγιος as angels (2.177 *Theod. Presb.* 18–22).

D. *Ir is called the holy assistance*: εἲρ . . . λέγεται ἁγία βοήθεια. If the author understands εἲρ as relating to the angel (cf. the OG reading), he regards the angel as a sign of God's assistance (cf. Dan 6:22; Bel 1:36). The expression ἅγια βοήθεια is rare (cf. *Mart. Jul. Basil.* 13.16; see Halkin, "Passion ancienne,"

The Sermon on the Demise of the Three Holy Youths

¹⁰Then Nebuchadnezzar, coming to his senses, sent peace to those who are near and those who are far away and^A appointed the holy^B Youths^C to be rulers over Babylon. After four months^D he fell asleep with faith in God.

Dan 4:33

Th. Dan 3:95–97

4 ¹After the end of the third kingdom from the resettlement^E of the children of Israel in Babylon^F another king arose of Persian lineage^G named Atticus. Having taken control over the kingdom of Babylon, he investigated the ranks of the Hebrews and became

---

256), but it most probably designates God's assistance, which is a much more widespread term (cf. LXX Ps 19:3; Judg 5:23; Jdt 8:17; 1 Macc 12:15; 2 Macc 12:11). There would be, however, some other interpretations of "Ir is called the holy assistance": (1) The Church Slavonic version of Hippolytus of Rome's *Comm. Dan.* 3.7.40 reads ἶρις (Slavonic *duga*; "rainbow") instead of ιρ (Bonwetsch, *Hippolytus*, 137; cf. Evseev, *Book of Daniel*, 70). This reading refers either to a rainbow as a sign of the covenant between God and Noah in Gen 9:13 (though the LXX uses τόξον instead of ἶρις) or to a rainbow over the head of the angel in Rev 10:1. If this reasoning is correct, it is possible that at earlier stages of the formation of the *Legend*, its author used a manuscript of Th. Dan in which עִיר (*'îr*) was translated as ἶρις instead of ιρ. Hebrew/Aramaic עִיר (*'îr*) looks similar to Hebrew עֵזֶר (*'ēzer*; "help," "assistance") and could be confused with it, since ʿ [y] can be mistaken for ז [z] when looked at inattentively or for someone who does not know Hebrew/Aramaic (I am grateful to Ivan Miroshnikov for this interesting suggestion). עֵזֶר (*'ēzer*) is sometimes rendered as βοήθεια in the LXX (e.g., LXX Ps 88:20). This confusion would somehow have been transmitted/known to the author of *Sermo de obit*. (3) if εἴρ is understood as "storm," the author may take "holy assistance" as an allusion on John 12:28–29: "Then a voice came from heaven, 'I have glorified it, and I will glorify it again.' The crowd standing there heard it and said that it was thunder. Others said, 'An angel has spoken to him.'"

A. D adds: "after they came out of the furnace of fire."

B. *holy*: D has "divine."

C. D adds: "with the prophet Daniel."

D. According to Dan 4:31–34, after Nebuchadnezzar's repentance and blessing of the Lord, his kingdom and health were returned to him for a while.

E. *resettlement*: D has "captivity."

F. *after the end . . . Babylon*: this remark seems to be a repetition of the beginning of ch. 3: "Now three kingdoms had changed in Babylon since the resettlement of the Hebrews" (3:1).

G. *arose of Persian lineage* (cf. *Mart. Dan.*): R has "was appointed." D calls this king "cruel and violent."

aware of their piety,^A more so of Daniel and the three holy Youths, and he ordered them to be arrested. ²Having set them upon the judgment platform, (the king) inquired about their wisdom. However, because of the sheer gravity of the platform,^B the guards around the throne, and the public boasting of punishment, the rest of the people shuddered.

³Then, the youngest Youth Misael, having received courage from God and having stretched out his hand in front of the king, began to say to him, "Although I am the youngest among my kindred Youths, because it is an abomination for them to answer you,^C I am compelled to say what concerns me, but first what concerns you. ⁴For so far, I answer to what concerns your violent and senseless desire, because you are worse than the wordless and creeping animals that are on the earth, and because the fire kindled through our lips you call god. ⁵You have a practice of eating together all kinds of food for dogs and wolves, for you are bound in a tribe to prosper for the purpose of cursed hypocrisy and you call fire a god which water extinguishes;^D therefore, you are also called Manichaeans. ⁶Henceforth stop, Atticus, whose name is lawless! For the prophet also calls you, saying, '*Whose sons are like young plants mature in their youth.*^E *Their daughters have been beautified. Their storehouses are full, bursting from side to side.*'^F ⁷*They counted happy the people to whom these things fall; no, but happy are the people, those whose God is the Lord.* We are those people, the humble workers.

⁸"Finally, I will tell you about us. We are children of^G pious rulers: father Hezekiah and mother Kallegonia. For our father Hezekiah dared to tell God, '*I have done the things that are pleasing in your sight,*' and he received the addition to his lifetime of fifteen more years. ⁹Our mother every day gave provisions,

Marginal references:
LXX Ps 143:12–13
LXX Ps 143:15
LXX 4 Kgdms 20:3, 6; LXX Isa 38:3, 5

A. *and became aware of their piety* (cf. *Mart. Dan.*): lacking in R.

B. *of the platform*: βήματος. D has βασιλέως (of the king). Cf. SlavR has "But since the king was quite obese."

C. D adds: "for they consider you an abomination" (cf. *Mart. Dan.*).

D. *eating together . . . extinguishes* (cf. *Mart. Dan.*): lacking in R.

E. *youth*: R has "profanity" (perhaps here "vanity").

F. *their storehouses . . . side*: lacking in D.

G. *we are children of*: D has "we were born of."

clothes, and money to those who begged, according to what they needed. And our father did the same as her, forgiving the tribute of the farmers in a time of scarcity of the cultivated lands, which he did during his kingship.

¹⁰"She testified to us that in due time the Word of God will come and open Hades . . . and that of Babylon and the restoring of Israel,^A the remains were hidden up to the time of the coming of our Master^B Christ until the venerable, glorious,^C and life-giving cross.^D

¹¹"When our Lord Jesus Christ was crucified, the foundations of the ground shook seeing the Immortal One hanging upon the cross;^E when heaven trembled, the sun darkened, the depths of^F abyss were confused; when the storehouses of Hades were illuminated^G and *many bodies of the saints who had fallen asleep were raised and entered the holy city*^H *and appeared to many,* ¹²among whom were Abel and Noah, as well as the Lord's other servants; then, those who previously witnessed about his appearance in flesh, the holy Youths and the all-wise Daniel, were raised. ¹³(Christ) brought them to his own and many others, more than 500 people, from the great number of those he had chosen and sent them to paradise, first his Holy Youths with their father Hezekiah and their good mentor Daniel. Those who had glorified him before his coming he sent to paradise; others he appointed to fall asleep a second time until his second coming. ¹⁴The bandit was a forerunner into paradise, the

Mark 15:33 par

Matt 27:51–53

A. Here Istrin's edition departs from the order of the manuscript pages, moving from fol. 64v to 65v.

B. *our Master*: D has: "in flesh."

C. *glorious*: lacking in D.

D. *Babylon . . . cross*: the Greek text is corrupted as a result of a displacement of material paralleling *Mart. Dan.* 5:6–9. In SlavR the sequence of events is intact and corresponds to *Mart. Dan.*

E. *when our Lord . . . cross*: D has "when the foundations of the ground shook" (cf. *Mart. Dan.*).

F. *depths of*: lacking in D.

G. *were illuminated* (cf. *Mart. Dan.*): D has "were caused to rock."

H. D is damaged at this point, with half of one column torn away. The text resumes at 4:15.

The Martyrdom of Daniel and the Three Youths

<small>Gen 3:24</small>
<small>Luke 23:43</small>

eleventh-hour[A] worker by the word of the Lord, which removed the flaming sword.[B] For when the Lord said to the bandit, '*you will be with me in*[C] *paradise*,' this word, having removed the flame of fire, brought the bandit to paradise. ¹⁵That is why Paul proclaimed, '*He appeared to more than five hundred brothers and sisters at one time, most of whom are still alive, though some have*

<small>1 Cor 15:6</small>

died.' Those he sent to paradise remain there until now, but to those whom he sent to fall asleep are . . .[D]

¹⁶"He will illuminate this plot of darkness. We also saw him, who appeared there[E] a little before this time, when we trampled the furnace[F] under the previous king,[G] who was, however, deemed worthy of salvation. ¹⁷But what will be with you in the

<small>Wis 3:7</small>

time of visitation? At that time, you will receive according to your deeds,[H] while we willingly accept death for the sake of Christ."

5 ¹Then, having consulted with his advisers about this answer, the king ordered the beheading of Misael. Having run up and stretched out his cloak,[I] Azarias received his head and cried. ²An-

---

A. *eleventh-hour worker*: this reading is based on SlavR; the Greek text lacks "eleventh." This is a reference to the repentant bandit (Luke 23:40–43), who is Jesus' forerunner to paradise. According to Luke, one of two bandits crucified with Jesus repents on the cross and asks Jesus to favor him when Jesus enters his kingdom. After the bandit's repentance, he is promised that he will attain the blessed reality of paradise immediately. *Sermo de obit.* 4:14 interprets how Jesus' promise has been fulfilled.

B. This alludes to the flaming sword at paradise's entrance in Gen 3:24. *Sermo de obit.* indicates that the repentant bandit could enter paradise because Jesus' word removed the flaming sword at its entrance (cf. *Gos. Nic.* 10).

C. Istrin's edition again departs from the order of the manuscript pages, moving from fol. 65v to 66r.

D. Beginning with the next phrase, the narrative returns to the point where Misael begins to speak of the coming of the Word of God (cf. *Mart. Dan.* 4:9–10).

E. *who appeared there*: lacking in D.

F. *when we trampled the furnace*: lacking in D.

G. In one last deviation from the order of the manuscript pages, Istrin's text moves from 66r to 65r.

H. *at that time . . . deeds*: D has "in the coming, terrifying judgement, you will receive punishment for your evil (deeds)."

I. *cloak*: φιλαπτόριον. This is a misspelled variant of φιβλατόριον (cf. *Mart. Dan.*).

gered, Atticus also ordered to behead Azarias. Hananias, having run up, enfolded both heads in his cloak. ³When Hananias also was stricken, Daniel stretched out his cloak^A on the ground and received their heads with weeping. He said, "Together we will go to the immortal king." And having bowed his precious neck, he was beheaded with his beloved and victorious martyrs.^B

⁴All the people of Israel ran up and mourned for them with great weeping, so that their grief filled the air. On the third day, having collected silver, they enlisted skilled silversmiths and fashioned coffins,^C engraving on each chest their own^D name. Taking the holy bodies, they put them down in the chests. Then, as everyone watched, each head was attached to its body. ⁵In the next night around midnight, they stole the bodies because Atticus sought to burn them. Together with their chests, they carried them to the mountain Gebal wishing to hide them. The rock set apart in itself and hid the remains of the holy ones.^E And after the return of the sons of Israel . . .^F

⁶From the good record,^G I, Cyril, the lowest^H bishop of the city of Alexandria, by means of the obtained account of Daniel^I

A. *cloak*: φιβλατόριον. It is περιβόλαιον (robe) in *Mart. Dan.* (cf. Deut 22:12).

B. *martyrs*: SlavU adds: "Instead of blood, milk came out of all those honest heads" (cf. *Men.*, fol. 335r). This remark is probably borrowed from the martyrdom account of another martyr (Istrin, *Alexandria*, 184). According to the *Acts of Paul* (14:5), a stream of milk flowed out from the wound on Paul's body after he was beheaded.

C. *coffins*: σωροθήκας. D has σαρκοθήκας ("tombs," "coffins"; cf. σαρκοφάγος).

D. *their own*: lacking in D.

E. *because Atticus . . . remains of the holy ones* (cf. *Mart. Dan.*): lacking in R.

F. The text here is broken as a result of the movement of the material corresponding to *Mart. Dan.* 5:6–9.

G. *from the good record*: ἐκ τῆς διαθήκης τῆς ἀγαθῆς. The Greek is unclear. It could be a mix of καὶ μετὰ τὴν ἐπάνοδον τῶν υἱῶν Ἰσραὴλ ἐκ Βαβυλῶνος ("after the return of the sons of Israel from Babylon") and ταύτην κατασκευὴν τῆς διαθήκης τῆς ἀγαθῆς ἐγὼ Κύριλλος . . . ("This version of the good record, I, Cyril . . .") as in M.

H. *lowest*: lacking in D.

I. *account of Daniel*: likely not a reference to a special text like the *Testament of Daniel* but to a certain tradition about him.

The Martyrdom of Daniel and the Three Youths

composed a brief story about the way of life and the departure in Christ of the holy and blameless Youths.[A] [7]May the flourished church of Christ bloom and advance in the fruit of righteousness by Christ's grace and the dignity of the perfectly commemorated glorious triumphant martyrs. Just as fathers and mothers make grow such plants with chastity[B] and piety, may young men and virgins increase in such goodness to be worthy of such a way of life. [8]The holy Youths departed on 17 December, by the grace and love for humanity of our Lord Jesus Christ, to whom is the glory and the power, forever and ever. Amen.

A. D adds: "the memories of the Holy Youths for the benefit of many."
B. *just as fathers . . . chastity*: lacking in D.

APPENDIX A

The Synaxarion and Chronicle Types of the Legend

1. Synaxarion of Constantinople

The Memory of the Three Holy Youths Hananias, Azarias, Misael, as well as the prophet Daniel. He (Daniel) was from the tribe of Judah from the family of the special royal service. He was born in upper Betharon.^A When he still was young, he was taken into the captivity from Judea to the Chaldean land. He prophesied for seventy years and foresaw Christ's birth four hundred years ahead. He was a temperate man, so that the Jews considered him to be a eunuch. He mourned a lot, lying on the ground, and practiced fasts, abstaining from any luxurious food. He was plain in appearance but very beautiful with the grace of the Most High. The Three Youths were, according to the received tradition, from the holy city of Jerusalem, from their father Hezekiah and their mother Kallegonia. This Hezekiah dared to tell God that he observed what is pleasing in God's sight. Then he received the addition of fifteen more years of life. When the Assyrian king Nebuchadnezzar besieged Jerusalem, they were led away to Babylon

Dan 1:3–6; Liv. Pro. 4:1

Liv. Pro. 4:2

2 Kgs 20:3, 6; Isa 38:3, 5
Dan 1:1

A. *was born in upper Betharon*: ἐγεννήθη δὲ ἐν Βηθαρῷ τῇ ἀνωτέρᾳ. According to Liv. Pro. 4:2, which is virtually copied here (ἐγεννήθη ἐν Βηθωρὼν τῇ ἀνωτέρᾳ), it is upper Beth-horon. Beth-horon was a city in the territory of Ephraim, on the way from Jerusalem to Joppa. There were two parts of the city, the upper and the lower Beth-horon (Josh 16:3, 5). In the LXX, Beth-horon MT בֵּית־חוֹרֹן [bēt-ḥôrōn] is transliterated either as Ωρωνίν (e.g., Josh 10:10) or Βαιθωρών (e.g., Josh 16:5).

The Martyrdom of Daniel and the Three Youths

Dan 2:48

Dan 3:1–23
Th. Dan 3:49–51

Dan 3:27–28

Dan 1:7; 4:9

as captives together with the prophet Daniel. There they were set as chiefs over the king's affairs because of their virtues. When they despised the idol which was set up, and did not worship it, they were thrown into a furnace that was burning seven times hotter than usual. There they sang praise, having been sprinkled with dew by the divine angel who came down to them. Then the king, having seen this marvelous thing, confessed the greatness of God, to whom they sang praises, for the furnace had turned to dew and the holy ones remained unharmed.[A] Although Daniel cohabited and lived with them and was the cause of their honor, he was not thrown into the furnace with them. Since this has been left silent in Scripture and remained unnoticed, it is perhaps, as it seems to me,[B] a sign of surpassing honor, which is not beyond the truth, because of the name Baltasar[C] given to him. For lest it should appear to those who revered fire as a god,[D] contrary to the established view, that their so-called god Baltasar had performed this marvelous wonder, Daniel, having received God's instruction, was not appointed to be thrown into the fire with them. This is why it is not recorded in the tale about the furnace.[E]

    A. The episode about the Son of God in the furnace (Th. Dan 3:91–92) is omitted in this version of the *Legend*.

    B. Such a personal and interpretative remark (see also "I suggest" at the end of the story) is unusual for quite formal Synaxarion texts.

    C. Βαλτάσαρ. Aramaic בֵּלְטְשַׁאצַּר (*bēlṭěšaʾṣṣar*) may have been interpreted as relating to the god Bel, but the etymology of this name is Akkadian and means "protect his life" (Collins, *Commentary*, 141).

    D. *revered fire as a God*: while *Mart. Dan.* and *Sermo de obit.* 4:4 reproach Atticus and the Persians in a similar way, here the author refers to the Babylonians.

    E. This explanation appears in Pseudo-John Chrysostom, *De tribus pueris et de fornace Babylonica* (*PG* 56:600). In the rabbinical tradition, after Daniel described Nebuchadnezzar's dream and interpreted it, the king paid him divine honors (cf. Dan 2:46). However, Daniel rejected such honor (*Gen. Rab.* 96.5). Furthermore, *b. Sanh.* 93a gives several reasons why Daniel was not with the Three Youths during the incident in the furnace: when Nebuchadnezzar set up a golden idol Daniel was not in Babylon because he was building a canal in Tiberias at that time; he was charged by the king to bring fodder for cattle; he had to bring the high-quality pigs from Alexandria of Egypt. *Shir. Rab.* 7.8, however, have Daniel in Babylon when the Three Youths were thrown into the furnace. See Ginzberg, *Legends of the Jews*, 2:1096–199.

The Three Holy Youths after their deliverance from the fire, which was beyond all reason, had been restored to what they were before and lived all their lives gloriously and passed away peacefully, along with Daniel.[A]

Dan 3:30
Dan 12:13

As some people tell, after the death of Nebuchadnezzar and other kings who honored the Three Youths and Daniel, another king arose, whose name was Atticus. He interrogated the holy ones and, having been reproached by them, ordered that Misael be beheaded. Stretching out his cloak, Azarias received (his head). In the same manner, Hananias received Azarias's cut off head, while Daniel, having spread out his clothes, received (Hananias's) head. Afterwards, his head also was cut off. It is told that after the beheading, each head was reattached to its body. The angel of the Lord took them and brought them to the mountain Gebal. They were placed there under the rock for four hundred years.[B] At the time of the resurrection of our Lord Jesus Christ they were also raised together[C] with him and passed away again.

The liturgical service[D] dedicated to them is commemorated in the Holy Great Church.[E] We have received (instruction) from our Fathers to commemorate their memory seven days before the Epiphany of the Master and the divine coming in flesh of our Lord, God, and Savior Jesus Christ. For they too, as I suggest, were from the tribe of Judah, the tribe from which Christ the Savior of all descended.

Dan 1:6

A. This first account of the deaths of Daniel and the Three Youths, the four men die peacefully and are presumably buried. There are several places where the burial place of Daniel was believed to be located: Shushan, Palestine, or Babylon; see Ginzberg, *Legends of the Jews*, 2:1115–18.

B. In contrast to 440 years in *Mart. Dan.* 5:10; SlavZ 5:10. Cf. Daniel's prediction of Christ's birth four hundred years ahead, referred to above.

C. *at the time of the resurrection . . . raised together*: this may be interpreted either as that they were resurrected at the same time Jesus was raised or that their resurrection relates to the event of Jesus' resurrection in general.

D. *liturgical service*: σύναξις.

E. *Holy Great Church*: the Hagia Sophia church in Constantinople; see Mateos, *Typicon*, 136. However, UkS 3:14 has "the great holy church of the Resurrection in Jerusalem."

The Martyrdom of Daniel and the Three Youths

2. Menologion of Basil II

The Contest of the Three Holy Youths, Hananiah, Azarias, and Misael

<small>2 Kgs 18:1–2
2 Kgs 20:3; Isa 38:3
2 Kgs 20:6; Isa 38:5
Dan 1:1–7
Dan 2:48
Dan 3:1–23
Th. Dan 3:49–51
Dan 3:28</small>

The Three Holy Youths were from the city of Jerusalem, the sons of Hezekiah, the king of the Jews. This Hezekiah dared to tell God that he observed that which is pleasing in God's sight. Having been deathly sick, he repented and received the addition of fifteen more years. When the Assyrian King Nebuchadnezzar besieged Jerusalem, they went to Babylon as captives. For their virtue they became the chiefs of that country. When they refused to worship the golden idol, which was made by the king, they were thrown into the furnace. And an angel came down and kept them unharmed. Then the king honored the Youths and confessed the greatness of the heavenly God. After this came another king who found that these Three Holy Youths believed in God and ordered to behead them. And the second received the head of the first and so on until the last one, Daniel, received the head of Hananias, and so they passed away.[A]

The Contest of the Holy Prophet Daniel

<small>Dan 1:12

Dan 2; 4

Dan 7–8; 11</small>

This holy Daniel was captured together with the Three Youths. He went to Babylon from Jerusalem and prophesied there for sixty years.[B] He foresaw Christ's birth four hundred and sixty years ahead.[C] He was a temperate and fasting man. He did not eat anything apart from vegetables. For this he was beloved by God. The angel was sent to teach him secrets.[D] Therefore he unraveled the king's dreams and interpreted them. He also prophesied about the kingdoms of all nations: the Medes, Assyrians, Persians, Macedonians, and Romans; that all kingdoms will be destroyed

---

A. In *Men. Basil II*, Daniel and the Three Youths are not resurrected.

B. *sixty*: seventy years in the Church Slavonic *Prolog* (Istrin, *Alexandria*, 180).

C. *four hundred and sixty years*: three hundred and sixty years in the Church Slavonic *Prolog* (Istrin, *Alexandria*, 180).

D. *secrets*: ἀπόκρυφα.

The Synaxarion and Chronicle Types

and the kingdom of the Romans[A] and Christians[B] will become the kingdom of Christ[C] himself forever.

Daniel was thrown to the den of lions and came out of it unharmed. He was honored as a son by King Belshazzar. Later, however, he (Daniel) was beheaded by King Atticus together with the Three Youths. — Dan 6; Bel 28–42; Dan 5:29

3. Greek Orthodox Menaion

17 December

Now he in reality sees you, the Divine, on the throne,

Having been beheaded, Daniel, but not in the dream as it was long ago. If the Three Youths had not chosen death, — Dan 11:33

As from the fire before, they would overcome the sword too.[D]

A. *the kingdom of the Romans*: according to Hippolytus of Rome, the Roman Empire will be the last kingdom in the world. The little horn that came up among the ten horns of the fourth beast (Dan 7:7–8) is the Antichrist. After his defeat the world will come to its end (*Comm. Dan.* 4.5.1–3). In *Men. Basil II*, the Antichrist is not mentioned at all.

B. *Christians*: Hippolytus of Rome relates Romans and Christians to each other: Jesus was born in the forty-second year of the reign of Caesar Augustus. His reign was the time of the flourishing of the Roman Empire (τὸ τῶν Ῥωμαίων βασίλειον). At the same time, the Lord established the people of the faithful Christians (ἔθνος πιστῶν χριστιανῶν) through the apostolic mission (*Comm. Dan.* 4.9.2–3). Probably, *Men. Basil II* identifies the Byzantine Empire with the Christian one. The Latin version of the *Apocalypse of Ps-Ephrem* states that at the end of time the kingdom of the Romans and Christians will be handed over to God the Father (*et iam regnum Romanorum tollitur de medio et Christianorum imperium traditur Deo et Patri*) (text in Caspari, *Briefe, Abhandlungen, und Predigten*, 213–14). Other Byzantine apocalyptic works indicate that the last Roman emperor will hand over his royal power to God (cf. 1 Cor 15:24); see Alexander, *Byzantine Apocalyptic Tradition*, 165.

C. *the kingdom of Christ*: in contrast to 1 Cor 15:24 and Rev 20:4, the kingdom is eternal and appears as a synonym of the kingdom of God. This is probably to harmonize with the Nicene-Constantinopolitan Creed: οὗ τῆς βασιλείας οὐκ ἔσται τέλος ("whose kingdom shall have no end").

D. The hymn underscores the desire of these righteous ones for martyrdom for Christ.

Daniel was beheaded on the seventeenth (of December), the one who sees the future.

4. The Second Edition of Slavonic Alexandria (*Alexandria*[2])

There is the tomb of the Three Youths and Daniel, whom King Nebuchadnezzar brought as captives from Jerusalem, near the city (of Babylon). For these Youths did not apostatize from their fathers' faith and were martyred with the sword by King Atticus. Each of them, having taken the head of the other, went out of the city into the mountains nearby and fell into eternal sleep.[A] Having come, the Chaldeans wanted to burn them with fire, and the rock split open and received their bodies; only their clothes were left.[B]

5. The Fourth Edition of Slavonic Alexandria (*Alexandria*[4])

About Daniel the prophet and the Three Youths. There are the tombs of the Three Youths and that of Daniel the prophet near the city (of Babylon). For they did not apostatize from their fathers' faith and were beheaded with the sword by King Atticus. Each of them, having taken the severed head of the other, went out of the city into the mountains nearby and fell into eternal sleep. Then the Chaldeans wanted to burn their bodies, but the rock split open and received their bodies; only their clothes were left.

A. In this version of the martyrdom, Daniel and his three companions not only receive the heads of each other, but also depart Babylon themselves, carrying their heads. This recalls the stories about the cephalophore martyrs, e.g., the legend about St. Aphrodisius who walked with his head to the place of his burial, or the martyrs Felix, Regula, and Exuperantius who picked up their heads after beheading and carried them forty paces uphill. It is interesting that neither *Alexandria*[2] nor *Alexandria*[4] speak about the resurrection of Daniel and the Three Youths.

B. A similar story is told of Thecla in the longer ending of the *Acts of Thecla*. She is chased by opponents into a cave; then she prays to God for help, and the wall of the cave opens. She enters the opening, leaving behind only a portion of her garment. For a discussion of these endings, see Jacobs, *Life of Thecla*, 13–14.

APPENDIX B

Further Development of the Legend in the Church Slavonic Tradition

1. Church Slavonic Manuscript from Zamość

1 ¹17 December: the martyrdom of the Three Holy Youths Hananias, Azarias, and Misael and the prophet Daniel. Lord, bless! I would like to proclaim a good tale to the churches of Christ about the courage of Christ's Youths and martyrs. Therefore, as much as you know God—more so, you are known by him—lend your ears   Gal 4:9
and truly listen, so that you can be deemed worthy to obtain the reward of the venerated martyrs. ²For it is necessary to praise and marvel at those who did not see the agony of death and the resurrection of the dead, but became confessors and martyrs before Christ's glorious coming in flesh. ³It is not we who proclaim to you about them, but it is the foresight of the precious prophecy, which has just been read to us. ⁴In that spirit, I would like to narrate the good story of the death of the kingly and kindred children Hannaias, Azarias, and Misael, together with the wise Daniel. Now, let us come and set the cornerstone of the ancient building, for which the most beautiful Youths of Jerusalem were appointed as bastions at the ends of the world.

⁵How do I bear witness to them? How shall I endure your acts and deeds? Crying out, I do not curse you; rather, conversing with you, I marvel at the word of command which God has spoken to you up to four times, testifying and saying through David, "*If your sons forsake my law and by my judgments do not*   LXX Ps 88:31

walk." ⁶He also threatens through Isaiah: "*Wash yourselves, become clean,* and *learn to do good.*" He also says, "*O Jerusalem, in you righteousness lodged, and now murderers!*" How is it sleeping? ⁷This is the offspring of the virgin, as David, foreseeing, cries, "*Rise up, O Lord, you and the ark of your sanctity. Your taverners mix the wine with water, your rulers are disobedient; they are companions of thieves.*" ⁷He also says through Micah, "*I will turn your feasts into mourning and will deport you beyond Babylon.*"

⁸When, therefore, you came into obedience,ᴬ the king of Assyria had already been sent against you, who, recalling the treasure under King Hezekiah, turned against you with an army. ⁹He brought the king of Assyria, who chose a horse tested from galloping many times into battles. A mighty young warrior, clad in armor, mounted the horse and shot (arrows) with both hands, not missing a single time. ¹⁰Then they attacked the city at the third hour of the night. At that time there was a great feast with many torches. There were round dancesᴮ and drunken parties, cymbals, and lyres, as well as the stomping of those who were dancing.ᶜ ¹¹Not only noble ones or free ones took part in this, but the whole city was gathered, every feasting assembly eating and drinking. ¹²Jeremiah went around, lamenting: "*How long until you will be quiet?* . . . . ¹³*like you have been locked . . . because (you are) their punishment and their deed.*"ᴰ The prophet

---

LXX Isa 1:16–17, 21

Isa 7:14
LXX Ps 131:8
Isa 1:22–23
Amos 5:27; 8:10

2 Kgs 18:13–37; Isa 36:1–22

2 Kgs 25:1; Hab 1:6–10; Dan 1:1

LXX Jer 29:6

A. *you came into obedience*: a misunderstood reading of καὶ οὐκ ἐπέμενες ἐν τῇ ὑπακοῇ ("and you did not persist in obedience") from manuscript P of *Mart. Dan.*

B. *round dances*: *lici*. This may be either a plural form of *lik* ("choir," "round dance"; cf. χοροί in *Mart. Dan.* 1:11) or a corrupted reading of *velicii* ("great ones"), as it says in *Men*. In the former case, the meaning of *lici i pirovĕ* is "partying and drinking."

C. *dancing*: *plačjuščich* ("crying") in the manuscript. This is most likely a scribe's mistake. The scribe mixed *pleščjuščich* ("dancing") with *plačjuščich* (see *Men.*; cf. ὀρχουμένων in *Mart. Dan.* 1:11).

D. The Slavonic text is corrupted and unclear. "Like you have been locked" may have come from "being locked in the chasm," while "their punishment and their deed" from "on account of their lawless action" in *Mart. Dan.* 1:13. Instead of "their punishment and their deed," *Men.* reads "their punished deed."

Appendix B: Further Development of the Legend

Abimelech was hidden outside the city^A so that he did not see the desolation of the city and the misfortune that suddenly occurred. ^14When the king of Babylon came, the trumpets buzzing in seven ranks with a great and heavy voice made an earthquake and iron-forged wheels of fire appeared, pummeling the walls into the ground. ^15The weapons were noisily clattering, warriors were fighting face-to-face, and the furious horses, whinnying with a barbarian noise, loudly roared. ^16All this produced a heavy thunder, so that the drunken parties suddenly stopped, and the torches were extinguished—as the prophet said, "*to change their feasts into mourning and their joy into lamentation.*" There was the collapse of the walls and of several buildings, and the burning of houses, and the fall of the corpses^B at the temple. ^17And their vessels for the worship, which were uncountable in the value of gold, and everything else were looted and brought out because of that unjust act.

4 Bar. 3:15–16; 5:1–2

Josh 6:16

LXX Amos 8:10

2 Kgs 24:10— 25:17; 2 Chr 36:17–20; Jer 52:12–23; Dan 1:2

2 ^1Then forty thousand men, women, and children were captured. The Assyrian (king) contrived to bind together a thousand men with one rope and in this manner brought the forty thousand out of their own city. ^2Among the multitude of the captives he set the Three Youths, who were born at the same time.^C In such a way, those (captives) who were ahead, were dragged through desolated places and woods with horse's bridles like donkeys and mules, while those who were behind were beaten to make them hurry up. ^3For (the king) commanded to lead them barefoot to their punishment, so that if one of them got caught on a thorn and wanted to tear the thorn out of his foot, the whole group of a thousand had to wait for the one, ^4because they were bound by the same rope. As David proclaimed, "*I was turned to wretchedness when a thorn was stuck in me.*" ^5Being so beaten, they went on foot and arrived at the third river of Babylon. Since their musical instruments were hung there on the tree, (the Babylonians) pressed them saying,

2 Kgs 24:16; 25:11; Jer 52:15

LXX Ps 31:4

A. *outside the city*: lit. "on the field." See the comment on *Mart. Dan.* 1:13.

B. *corpses*: "pillars" in *Men*.

C. *born at the same time*: *edinorodnyę* (literally, "the only children"). UkS also has "born at the same time" (1:1 and the marginal note to 3:13).

The Martyrdom of Daniel and the Three Youths

"Sing us a psalm in the same way you did in your land!" ⁶At that moment, the Three Youths, who were born at the same time, stood up and said, "It is inappropriate to speak the words of God before the wicked one." They were then beaten by a knotted rod until the ninth hour of that day. The blameless Youths said, "Let us praise the Lord in secret."

⁷The next morning, at the third hour, the humanity-loving and gentle God recalled the covenant made with Abraham. ⁸At the entreaty of these righteous ones, he sent them healing angels to heal his people from the torment of the lawless, and having calmed the adversaries, he turned their hearts to mercy. ⁹After that, the king of Babylon saw a dream which was hard to explain, and through the wise Daniel and the holy Youths he learned the meaning of the dream. On this account, he appointed them to be the rulers of the whole country.

3 ¹Three kings had changed (in Babylon) since the resettlement of the Hebrews, but their mind had not changed, nor had they joined the faithless people and participated in their profanities ²The three venerable Youths followed along with their good mentor (Daniel) and smashed the sixty-cubit vainglorious image, and by striking it, they killed the sixty-cubit dragon, who was regarded as a god. ³These writings of the holy ones were found written on crystal plates. For this reason, I thought it necessary to tell you their extraordinary and completely unknown story.

⁴After the images of the vainglorious gods were smashed by the power of these holy men, it was contrived, at the devil's advice and envy, to prepare for them a furnace of fire. However, God sent the archangel Michael, so that when they were thrown into the furnace, the angel of God could cool them down. All day and night they were chilled and rejoiced in the middle of the fire. ⁵Their hair was kept unburned, and their faces were unchanged, while their feet were as if they were walking on drops of dew, because the Spirit of the Lord was cooling them down.

⁶For this reason, the king said, "Did we not throw the three men into the furnace? Now I see four, and the appearance of the fourth is as if he were the Son of God!"

Appendix B: Further Development of the Legend

⁷Azarias said to him, "Tell me, O King, impious and mad, how you, not knowing God, can proclaim the Son of God? For his sake, we have chosen every kind of torment, so that when he who is in human flesh through the pure Virgin comes to us here, as it is written, he may appoint us his servants to be his witnesses in the future." LXX Isa 7:14; 8:8

⁸Then, the king said, "And I see the light descending." Th. Dan 4:13

⁹Azarias said, "Do you not realize that the fear of God is making you see even the Holy of Holies?"

¹⁰Then Nebuchadnezzar, gripped by fear, understood, and believed this. He ran up to the furnace, bowed down before them, and said to them, "Hananias, Azarias, and Misael, come out from the furnace! For I have realized that there is no other god who could have done this, who has turned the furnace cold." And he added, "Anybody who utters blasphemy against the living God, shall be destroyed!" (The king) sent (a message) to those who were near and who were far away and appointed the Youths to be rulers over Babylon. After this, he fell asleep with faith in God. Th. Dan 3:93–97

4 ¹Four months after his death, another king arose there. He was of Persian lineage named Atticus, who ruled over the kingdom for thirty-four years and inquired about the Babylonian decrees. When he became aware of the virtue of the holy men Daniel and the Three Youths, ²he asked them, "What is the wisdom of the Hebrews and whose parents do they[A] happen to be descendants of?" His throne was surrounded by imposing servants who instilled fear in all who were present. But the Holy Youths stood (there) bravely, waving their hands in the air.

³Then Misael began to answer the king, "I am the youngest among those Youths who are like me, but who previously did not want to talk to you, because they consider it to be an abomination to speak with you and about you. ⁴I, however, will respond to you, to a mind incapable of understanding counsel. You are like crawling and poisonous animals, which kindle fire in their mouths and then extinguish it, ⁵while you regard yourself as a dog or a wolf. ⁶So it is given to your kind and to your tribe to prosper on earth to the condemnation of the curse, as

---

A. *they*: likely a mistaken reading for "you," as in *Mart. Dan.*

did Makidon,^A your father, who for the sake of unjust wealth let himself be married to Sirens.^B ⁷And so, at the instigation and screech of the unclean spirit, you have learned to kill the Jews and to destroy the offspring of their cattle by fire. You regard the unlawful blending as a sacrifice. Mixing their blood with blood, you do not realize that you are eating your own flesh, and therefore you are called Manichaeans.

⁸"Well, now our names will be told. We are children of pious parents, father Hezekiah and mother Kaligona, who dared to say to God, '*I have done the things that are pleasing in your sight, walked before you in truth*,' who then received from God an addition of fifteen more years, and who had forgiven the tribute to the tillers of the land. ⁹He is the one who prophesied to us that in due time, the Word of God will come in the form of a human being, who will open hell and illuminate the darkness. (This Word) we saw as an image even before that time, when we trampled fire during the rule of the king before you. ¹⁰However, he was deemed worthy

<small>LXX 4 Kgdms 20:3, 6; LXX Isa 38:3, 5</small>

A. *Makidon*: *Makidonŭ*. It looks like a transliterated version of Μακεδών. In the LXX, Μακεδών is used for Haman in Esth 8:12 (Αμαν Αμαδαθου Μακεδών); 9:24 (Αμαν Αμαδαθου ὁ Μακεδών); and for Alexander the Great in 1 Macc 6:2 (Ἀλέξανδρος . . . ὁ βασιλεὺς ὁ Μακεδών). It is doubtful that *Zamoscia* refers to either of these two characters. Perhaps its author or editor simply read and then translated Μαγεδών as *Makidonŭ*, which sounds similar to *Magedonŭ*. However, it is also probable that he understood the name *Makidonŭ* (literally, "Macedonian") more anachronistically as a distorted version of the name Macedonius, which was used in a negative context. This may refer to Macedonius I, the bishop of Constantinople (4th cent.), who established the heretical ante-Nicene Creed sect of Macedonians or *Pneumatomachi* ("the fighters against the Spirit"). Moreover, the name Atticus could have been taken by SlavZ as that of Atticus (Ἀττικός), the archbishop of Constantinople (5th cent.). He succeeded John Chrysostom in the See of Constantinople and, at first, was in opposition to his predecessor, but after the death of Chrysostom became a supporter of his views. This Atticus was born at Sebaste in Armenia and became a monk when he was still a young man. He received his first monastic education from certain monks who adhered to the sect of Macedonians and lived near him. Only later he became Orthodox (see Wace and Piercy, *Dictionary*, 69). If the author or editor of SlavZ knew this Atticus's biography, he may have metaphorically incorporated it into the story: King Atticus is like the archbishop Atticus for whom Macedonius of Constantinople was a kind of spiritual father. It may mean that Atticus is portrayed as a heretic like the Macedonians and Manichaeans (Somov, "Martyrdom of Daniel," 217).

B. *Sirens*: *Sirinami*. Cf. Σειρῆνες/Συρίνες ("Sirens" or "deceitful women").

of salvation, whereas in the days of salvation, you will realize that what you wanted to do to us will be done to you."

5 ¹The king became fiercely angry at this answer and, having consulted (with his advisers), he ordered the beheading of Misael. Having run up, Azarias stretched out his clothes, received his head, and cried. ²But Atticus also ordered to behead Azarias. Then, Hananias, having run up, received both heads in a cloak and said, "We will go together to the Lord and Savior of the whole world." ³Bowing his head, he also was beheaded. Then, having stretched out his robe on the ground, Daniel received the heads of the three, and, kneeling down, was also beheaded.

⁴All Israel mourned for them with great weeping. Then they hid their bodies and buried them. They brought a skilled goldsmith who made coffins and engraved on each one the names (of those who were laid there) and placed the bodies therein. Suddenly, their heads joined each to its own body. ⁵Since the king wanted to burn their bodies, the angels took them at night to Mount Egeval to hide them there. Suddenly, the rock split and hid the bodies of the saints. After the return of the children of Israel and the restoration of Jerusalem, the bodies of the saints were in Babylon until the time of the coming of the Master in the flesh.

⁶When the Jews set up the Cross against our Lord Jesus Christ, the foundations of the ground shivered at seeing God being given over to the grave; heaven shook, rocks were broken in pieces, the tops of mountains trembled. When all of hell was illuminated, *many bodies of the saints who had fallen asleep were raised and having entered the holy city appeared to many.* ⁷Among them were Abel, Noah, Abraham, Isaac, Jacob, Joseph, Isaiah, Jeremiah,[A] Hezekiah with his wife and with their own three children Hananias, Azarias, and Misael, and their mentor Daniel, John the Forerunner of Christ, and a great multitude of others. ⁸The Master chose many of them and sent them to paradise. Others he commanded to fall asleep again until his second coming. ⁹This is why Paul says, "*He appeared to more than five hundred brothers and sisters at one time, most of whom still remain,*" that

Matt 27:51–53

1 Cor 15:6

A. Baruch is omitted from this list as well as in the episode of Jeremiah's mourning over Jerusalem in 1:13 (cf. *Sermo de obit.* 1:13).

is "remain in paradise," but those whom he has let fall asleep are asleep. This came about as a result of the resurrection.[A]

¹⁰Therefore, having so suffered, the Three blameless Youths were preserved in the rock for 440 years. Then they were raised and were settled in their own place, by the grace and love for humanity of the Father, the Son, and the Holy Spirit, now and forever and unto the ages of ages. Amen.

2. The Ukrainian Manuscript of the Priest Stephen Teslevtsiv

1 ¹On the same day: the memory of the Three Holy Youths Hananias, Azarias, and Misael. These Three Holy Youths or boys were sons of Hezekiah, the king of Jerusalem, and their mother's name was Kaligoria. These boys were born at the same time and were very beautiful. ²When they were fifteen years old, they were taken into captivity together with Daniel. ³When the Babylonians captured Jerusalem, the Babylonian King Nebuchadnezzar took them (into his service) because of their beauty and wisdom, as well as because they were from a great royal family. ⁴King Nebuchadnezzar loved them very much and appointed them the rulers of the country of Babylon. ⁵Their names were: the first one is Hananias, the second one Azarias, and the third one is Misael. However, the king gave them other names, according to his country and his language. ⁶He renamed Hananias to Sedrach, Azarias to Meshach,[B] and Misael to Abdenago.[C] These Three Youths were well-trained in writing.

⁷When they were brought to Babylon, one day King Nebuchadnezzar put together a feast and commanded the Three Youths to play and sing the songs of their country in front of them, because at that time there were excellent royal musicians, as well as various singers. ⁸The king arranged this feast above the Babylonian River called Asidon. But the Three Youths were in

2 Kgs 18:1–2

Dan 1:3–6; Isa 39:7

Dan 1:7

A. *this came about ... resurrection*: cf. γένονε δὲ ταῦτα διὰ τὴν πρᾶξιν τῆς ἀναστασίας (*Mart. Dan.* 5:9 manuscripts P and B).

B. *Azarias ... Abdenago*: the new names for Azarias and Misael are mixed up: Azarias had to be Abdenago and Misael Meshach.

C. *Abdenago*: Avŭdenij.

Appendix B: Further Development of the Legend

great distress because they were in captivity and (yet) they (still) had to sing the songs of Zion. ⁹There, before the king and all the nobles, the three princes began to sing the psalm of the holy prophet David, saying through the Holy Spirit, "*By the rivers of Babylon, Halleluia, there we sat and wept remembering Zion, Halleluia.*" ¹⁰They recalled the land of Jerusalem and sang a lament. This simply means, "Sitting on the low banks of the Babylonian river, we sing beautiful songs, recalling the cities of Zion. ¹¹What should we do now, brothers? We must lament, hanging our useless lutes, that is, musical instruments, on the willows."

¹²And they hung their instruments on a willow over the river of Sidon and began to sing a very pitiful and beautiful song: "O, our heavenly God, what should we do? Who can listen to the sound of your songs in the pagan land?" ¹³For the Babylonians were pagans. Babylon is a pagan city; Chaldeans, Babylonians, pagans—it is all the same. ¹⁴Then they sang again: "They burned our place, broke down the walls, and defiled your holy temple. Some people have been killed, others have been taken into captivity, and the walls have collapsed to their foundation." ¹⁵The king commanded his soldiers, "Raze it, raze it, even to its foundations!" They say again, "O, Lord, where is your word that you said: *If I forget you, O Jerusalem, may my right hand be forgotten.* You swore, O Lord, with your tongue and said, *May my tongue stick in my throat, if I do not remember you*, O Jerusalem; *if I do not set Jerusalem at the beginning of my gladness.* ¹⁶Do not forget us, God, and your holy place! What has she done to us, wicked daughter of Babylon, the shameless wench, the damned harlot! But you also, O glorious Babylon, seat of the Chaldeans, be on guard and believe carefully, for you see a destruction looming over your head. ¹⁷Blessed and strong is a man who rewards you for us and who dashes your evil and miserable sons against the rock."

¹⁸Then what happened out there, by God's will? They were singing, but their violins were hanging on the willows and yet they still beautifully accompanied their song, so that all the pagans marveled. ¹⁹And David's prophecy was fulfilled there. And as concerns the lamentation by the river of Babylon, read the eighth kingly book, chapter six and you will learn about the

References (margin):
LXX Ps 137:1
2 Chr 36:17–20; LXX Ps 73:7; 78:1–3; Jer 52:12–14
LXX Ps 136:7
LXX Ps 136:5–6
LXX Ps 136:8
LXX Ps 136:9

sacking of Jerusalem.^A ^20 This prophecy has also been fulfilled about the decline and desolation of Babylon. For Babylon has now been desolated and destroyed, while Jerusalem stands glorious until today.

^21 And so King Nebuchadnezzar loved these Three Boys and Daniel very much and always held them in great favor. He appointed them chiefs over the entire country of Babylon.

2 ^1 King Nebuchadnezzar then made a very large and expensive golden idol sixty cubits high and set it up in the glorious plain of Deira.^B He commanded all the people from his entire kingdom to gather there. ^2 He also gathered musical instruments, various pipes, trumpets, fifes, and every kind of music that exists in the world for comfort to be played, sounded, blown, and sung before that god and ordered that in the time when the people heard that sound they should fall down to the ground before that golden idol and worship it, praising and glorifying it as God. ^3 What then happened upon the king's command? At that time the Three Youths did not want to worship that golden idol and scorned it, since it was not God: "O, your majesty, we believe in the heavenly God, who created heaven and earth, as well as this world and everything in it. This, O King, is the God who exists, but your golden idol is not God. We do not want to and will not bow down to him."

^4 When King Nebuchadnezzar heard this, he was very angry with them and commanded that all Three be thrown alive into a fiery furnace, into a great fire, having made a strong fire in this Chaldean furnace. ^5 It was set up there for this reason: if anyone did not kneel and worship the golden idol that King Nebuchadnezzar had set up, he or she should be cast into the fiery furnace. It was burning hot, seven times seven. ^6 The Three beautiful Boys were cast into it, born brothers from the same father and mother, faithful servants of God the Sabaoth, in all

---

A. As Franko (*Collected Works*, 261) indicates, Teslevtsiv did not know the Bible well and often provided references to sections of books that do not exist in the Bible (e.g., Exod 42) or misattributed certain stories to biblical books that do not contain those stories. Here the author probably means what is said in 2 Kgs 25:11–17.

B. *Deira*: cf. Δεῖρα in Th. Dan 3:1, דּוּרָא (*dûraʾ*) in MT Dan 3:1.

APPENDIX B: FURTHER DEVELOPMENT OF THE LEGEND

their precious garments. ⁷They sang there a song to the heavenly God and the holy Michael immediately came down to them to this powerful fiery furnace. ⁸The flame was enormous—forty-nine cubits higher than that furnace. The angel of the Lord came and cooled them down. ⁹There was a noise in that furnace as if a cold wind was blowing and they were walking in the furnace as if in a bath. Not a single hair on their head did perish; not one was scorched. ¹⁰What happened there by the heavenly God's power? The fire fell out of the furnace, turned around, and scorched those unbelievers who were near the furnace. ¹¹The flame began to scorch the Chaldeans, those pagan Babylonians, and Nebuchadnezzar himself barely escaped from there.^A Then many gentiles began to believe in the heavenly God. ¹²The king commanded to take the Three Youths out from the furnace. Then the king treated them even better and honored them more. ¹³And at last, King Nebuchadnezzar himself believed in the heavenly God because the Lord God punished King Nebuchadnezzar so much that he became like an ox and ate grass for six years,^B and then he became a man again. ¹⁴After this, the Three Youths lived for many years in peace and everyone feared them as they feared King Nebuchadnezzar himself.

Dan 3:1–23
Th. Dan 3:24
Th. Dan 3:47–50
Dan 3:27

Th. Dan 3:48

Dan 3:26

Dan 3:28–29
Dan 4:29–37

3 ¹It is written about them and told in some ancient books, that when King Nebuchadnezzar and other great noble ones, who honored and respected Daniel and those Three Youths, died, another king arose, named Atticus. He was a wicked and unfaithful king and he hated Daniel and the Three Youths. ²He commanded to summon them to him and began to force and convince them to abandon the one God and to worship his pagan gods. But they stood firm in their faith and did not want to submit to his will. ³They blasphemed his gods and reproached the king himself. King Atticus grew angry and ordered them to be beheaded. ⁴For the wicked always hates the good through the instigation of the devil. Indeed Satan himself is at war there,

---

A. *Nebuchadnezzar . . . from there*: this detail is added by the editor of this version of the *Legend*.

B. *six years*: "seven times (וְשִׁבְעָה עִדָּנִין) [*wĕšibʿâ ʿiddānîn*]" in MT Dan 4:13, 29.

because he himself is wicked, and he wants all people to love him in his wickedness, and to do his satanic will, and to hate the good. ⁵For so it is now in this world of profanity: Satan loves Satan, and the evil one loves the evil one, praising and flattering his evil deeds. The rich one hates the poor one, the lawless one hates the truthful one, the unmerciful one hates the merciful one, and the wicked godless one hates the pious one. ⁶The sinner judges, taunts, reproaches, and mocks the righteous one. The wicked one does not want to hear the word of God, but he is angry with the one who instructs him in the good way, and berates and hates him. ⁷And all this is because Satan drives him to it, so he does not have to sit in hell by himself. It used to be that the wicked one disliked the good one, and it is the same now. But in the end, such people will suffer sorrow!

⁸What happened then to the holy Daniel and those Three Youths, who were true-born brothers and chiefs? First, the faithless King Atticus ordered Misael's head to be cut off. ⁹When his head was cut off, Hananias took it in his hands and kissed it affectionately. While holding this head, holy Hananias was beheaded and Azarias took his head in his hands and kissed it affectionately, shedding tears. And while holding that head, Azarias was beheaded too. ¹⁰Then, holy Daniel spread out Hananias's cloak,^A laid Azarias's head on it, kissed it affectionately, and prayed^B to the Lord God of heaven. ¹¹Afterwards, holy Daniel was also beheaded with a sword because King Atticus was angry with Daniel for smashing his god and killing his priests.^C For this, he ordered Daniel to be beheaded.

¹²It is written that Saint Michael came and attached all four heads to their bodies. He took them from that pagan country and brought them to Mount Gebal, in their own country,^D and laid them under the foot of a certain rock. ¹³But after four hundred years, when Christ had risen, they also were raised and appeared

---

A. In this version of the *Legend*, Daniel uses Hananias's cloak to receive Azarias's head.

B. *prayed*: lit. "spoke various words."

C. Here Atticus is confused with King Astyages from the story about Bel and the Dragon.

D. Teslevtsiv definitely localizes Gebal in Israel.

Appendix B: Further Development of the Legend

to many people and spoke to all who saw them. Then they were carried invisibly into the holy paradise.^A   Matt 27:52–53

¹⁴Their holy memory is commemorated in the great holy church of the Resurrection in Jerusalem, for it is written: a great church.^B For the Holy Fathers had decided to commemorate their memory seven days before the Nativity. ¹⁵Through the prayers of these (righteous ones), O Christ our God, have mercy on us always, now and forever, and unto the ages of ages. Amen.

A. In the margins of the manuscript: "They were from the tribe of Judah and were born at the same time" (cf. UkS 1:1).

B. *the great church*: Teslevtsiv mistakenly regards it as the church of the Holy Sepulchre in Jerusalem instead of the Hagia Sophia church in Constantinople.

Bibliography

Texts and Translations

Bayan, George, ed. "Le Synaxaire arménien de Ter Israël." *PO* 18 (1924) 5–208.
Bonwetsch, Gottlieb N., ed. *Hippolytus: Die Kommentare zu Daniel und zum Hohenliede*. GCS 1,1. Leipzig: Hinrichs, 1897.
Botvinnic, M. N., Y. S. Lourye, and O. V. Tvorogov, eds. *Alexandria: A Novel About Alexander of Macedon According to a 15th Century Russian Manuscript*. Leningrad: Nauka, 1965.
Bovon, François, and Christopher R. Matthews, trans. *Acts of Philip: A New Translation*. Waco, TX: Baylor University Press, 2012.
Budge, E. A. Wallis, trans. *The Book of the Saints of the Ethiopian Church: A Translation of the Ethiopic Synaxarium: Made from the Manuscripts Oriental 660 and 661 in the British Museum*. 4 vols. Cambridge: Cambridge University Press, 1928.
Caspari, C. P., ed. *Briefe, Abhandlungen, und Predigten aus den zwei letzten Jahrhunderten des kirchlichen Alterthums und dem Anfang des Mittelalters*. Brussels: Mallingsche Buchdruckerei, 1890.
Delehaye, Hippolyte, ed. *Synaxarium ecclesiae Constantinopolitanae e codice Sirmondiano nunc Berolinensi adiectis synaxariis selectis*. Brussels: Société des Bollandistes, 1902.
De Vis, Henri, ed. *Homélies Coptes de la Vaticane*. 2 vols. Copenhagen: Gyldendal, 1922–29.
Dmitry of Rostov. *The Lives of the Saints*. Vol. 2: *December, January, February*. Kyiv: Kyiv Pechersk Lavra, 1764 (in Church Slavonic).
Drijvers, H. J. W., ed. and trans. *The Book of the Laws of Countries: Dialogue on Fate of Bardaiṣan of Edessa*. 1964. Reprint, Piscataway, NJ: Gorgias, 2007.
Eastman, David L., trans. "The Epistle of Pseudo-Dionysius the Areopagite to Timothy Concerning the Deaths of the Apostles Peter and Paul." In *New Testament Apocrypha: More Noncanonical Scriptures*, edited by Tony Burke and Brent Landau, 1:64–80. Grand Rapids: Eerdmans, 2016.
Elliott, J. K., trans. *The Apocryphal New Testament: A Collection of Apocryphal Christian Literature in an English Translation*. Oxford: Oxford University Press, 1993.
Franchi de'Cavalieri, Pio, ed. *Il menologio di Basilio II: Cod. Vaticano greco*. 2 vols. Turin: Fratelli Bocca, 1907.
Franko, Ivan, ed. *Apocrypha and Legends from Ukrainian Manuscripts*. Vol. 1: *The Old Testament Apocrypha*. Lviv: Shevchenko, 1896 (in Ukrainian).

BIBLIOGRAPHY

Garitte, Gérard, ed. *Le calendrier palestino-géorgien du Sinaiticus 34 (Xe Siècle).* Subsidia Hagiographica 30. Brussels: Société des Bollandistes, 1958.

———, ed. and trans. "L'invention géorgienne des trois enfants de Babylone." *Mus* 72 (1959) 69–100.

———, ed. and trans. "Le texte arménien de l'invention des trois enfants de Babylone." *Mus* 74 (1961) 91–108.

Ginzberg, Louis. *Legends of the Jews.* 2 vols. Translated by Henrietta Szold and Paul Radin. 1909–38. 2nd ed. Philadelphia: Jewish Publication Society, 2003.

Goldstein, Jonathan A. *II Maccabees: A New Translation with Introduction and Commentary.* AB 41A. New York: Doubleday, 1983.

Herzer, Jens, ed. and trans. *4 Baruch (Paraleipomena Jeremiou).* WGRW 22. Atlanta: Society of Biblical Literature, 2005.

Hill, Edmund, trans. *The Works of Saint Augustine: A Translation for the 21st Century.* Vol. 3.8: *Sermons 273–305A on the Saints.* Edited by John Rotelle. Hyde Park, NY: New City, 1994.

Istrin, V. M. *Alexandria in Russian Chronographs.* Moscow: Moscow State University Press, 1893 (in Russian).

———. "Greek Copies of the Apocryphal Martyrdom of Daniel and the Three Youths." *Collected Articles of the Department of Russian Language and Literature* 70 (1901) 1–18 (in Russian).

———. *History of Serbian Alexandria in Russian Literature.* Vol. 1. Odessa: Economicheskaya, 1909 (in Russian).

Jacobs, Andrew S., trans. *The Life of Thecla: Apocryphal Expansion in Late Antiquity.* Early Christian Apocrypha 11. Eugene, OR: Cascade Books, 2024.

James, M. R., ed. *The Lost Apocrypha of the Old Testament: Their Titles and Fragments.* Translations of Early Documents: Palestinian Jewish Texts (Pre-Rabbinic) 1. London: SPCK, 1920.

Jerome. *The Principal Works of St. Jerome.* Vol. 6. Translated by M. A. Freemantle. Edited by Philip Schaff and Henry Wace. NPNF[2]. Grand Rapids: Hendrickson, 1995.

Kuhn, K. H., ed. and trans. "A Coptic Jeremiah Apocryphon." *Mus* 83 (1970) 95–135, 291–350.

Likhachev, D. S., et al., eds. *Library of Ancient Russian Literature.* Vol. 8: *14th–First Half of the 16th Century.* St. Petersburg: Nauka, 2003 (in Russian).

Macarius, Metropolitan of Moscow. *The Great Menaion Reader.* 16 vols. St. Petersburg: Archaeographic Commission, 1868–1915 (in Russian).

Mateos, Juan, ed. and trans. *Le typicon de la Grande Église. Ms. Sainte-Croix no. 40, X Siècle. Introduction, texte critique, traduction et notes.* Vol. 1: *Le cycle des douze mois.* OrChrAn 165. Roma: Pont. Institutum Orientalium Studiorum, 1962.

Migne, Jacques-Paul. *Patrologiae cursus completus: Series graeca.* Vol. 77. Paris: Cerf, 1864 (partial text, cols. 1117–18).

Μηναῖον τοῦ Δεκεμβρίου. Venice: Fenix, 1863.

Μηναῖον τοῦ Δεκεμβρίου. Athens: Apostolic Ministry of the Greek Church, 2018.

Μηναῖον τοῦ Νοεμβρίου. Venice: Fenix, 1889.

Musurillo, Herbert, ed. *The Acts of the Christian Martyrs.* Oxford: Clarendon, 1972.

Bibliography

Robinson, Steve. "4 Baruch: A New Translation and Introduction." In *The Old Testament Pseudepigrapha*. Vol. 2: *Expansions of the "Old Testament" and Legends, Wisdom and Philosophical Literature, Prayers, Psalms, and Odes, Fragments of Lost Judeo-Hellenistic Works*, edited by James H. Charlesworth, 413–25. Garden City, NY: Doubleday, 1985.

Somov, Alexey B. "The Martyrdom of Daniel and the Three Youths in the Slavonic Tradition." In *Old Slavonic Evidence of Parabiblical Literature: History and Eschatology*, edited by Tomás García-Huidobro and Alexey B. Somov, 164–87. Moscow: St. Thomas Institute, 2024 (in Russian) (excerpts, pp. 169–79).

Stone, Michael E., ed. and trans. *Armenian Apocrypha from Adam to Daniel*. EJL 55. Atlanta: SBL, 2021.

———. *Armenian Apocrypha Relating to the Patriarchs and Prophets*. Jerusalem: Israel Academy of Sciences and Humanities, 1982.

———. "An Armenian Tradition Relating to the Death of the Three Companions of Daniel." *Mus* 86 (1973) 111–23.

Tichonravov, Nikolai S., ed. *Documents of Renounced Russian Literature*. Vol. 1. St. Petersburg: Partnership "Public benefit," 1863 (in Russian).

Vassiliev, Athanasius, ed. *Anecdota Graeco-Byzantina: pars prior*. Moscow: Sumptibus et typis Universitatis Caesareae, 1893.

Ziegler, Joseph, trans. *Septuaginta: Vetus Testamentum Graecum*. Vol. 16.2: *Sussana, Daniel, Bel et Drago*. Göttingen: Vandenhoeck & Ruprecht, 1954.

Studies and Other Works Cited

Albl, Martin C. "Ancient Christian Authors on Jews and Judaism." In *The "New Testament" as a Polemical Tool: Studies in Ancient Christian Anti-Jewish Rhetoric and Beliefs*, edited by Riemer Roukema and Hagit Amirav, 15–56. NTOA/SUNT 118. Göttingen: Vandenhoeck & Ruprecht, 2018.

Alexander, Paul J. *The Byzantine Apocalyptic Tradition*. Berkeley: University of California Press, 1985.

Allen, Leslie C. *Psalms 101–150*. WBC 21. Dallas, TX: Word, 2002.

Allison, Dale C. *4 Baruch (Paraleipomena Jeremiou)*. CEJL. Berlin: de Gruyter, 2019.

Antonini, Luciana. "Le chiese cristiane nell'Egitto dal IV al IX secolo secondo i documenti dei papiri greci." *Aegyptus* 20.3 (1940) 129–208.

Barr, James. *The Typology of Literalism in Ancient Biblical Translations*. Mitteilungen des Septuaginta-Unternehmens 15. Göttingen: Vandenhoeck & Ruprecht, 1979.

Bledsoe, Amanda M. Davis. "The Relationship of the Different Editions of Daniel: A History of Scholarship." *CurBR* 13.2 (2015) 175–90.

Bons, Eberhard. "The Septuagint and Greek Style." In *T&T Clark Handbook of Septuagint Research*, edited by William A. Ross and W. Edward Glenny, 93–108. London: T. & T. Clark, 2021.

Borg, Marcus J., and John Dominic Crossan. *The Last Week: What the Gospels Really Teach About Jesus's Final Days in Jerusalem*. New York: HarperCollins, 2006.

Bovon, François. "Beyond the Canonical and the Apocryphal Books, the Presence of a Third Category: The Books Useful for the Soul." *HTR* 105 (2012) 125–37.

Bibliography

———. "'Useful for the Soul': Christian Apocrypha and Christian Spirituality." In *The Oxford Handbook of Early Christian Apocrypha*, edited by Andrew Gregory and Christopher Tuckett, 185–95. New York: Oxford University Press, 2015.
Bradshaw, Paul F., and Maxwell E. Johnson. *The Origins of Feasts, Fasts and Seasons in Early Christianity*. Alcuin Club Collections 86. Collegeville, MN: Liturgical, 2011.
Brakmann, Heinzgerd, et al. "Jünglinge im Feuerofen." *RAC* 19 (1999) 346–88.
Buchinger, Harald. "Die vielleicht älteste erhaltene Predigt auf das Epiphaniefest: Vier syrische Fragmente des Titus von Bostra (CPG 3578)." In *Synaxis katholike: Beiträge zu Gottesdienst und Geschichte der fünf altkirchlichen Patriarchate für Heinzgerd Brakmann zum 70 Geburtstag*, edited by Diliana Atanassova and Tinatin Chronz, 1:65–86. Orientalia-patristica-oecumenica 6.1. Vienna: Lit, 2014.
Bucur, Bogdan Gabriel. "Christophanic Exegesis and the Problem of Symbolization: Daniel 3 (the Fiery Furnace) as a Test Case." *Journal of Theological Interpretation* 10.2 (2016) 227–44.
———. *Scripture Re-Envisioned: Christophanic Exegesis and the Making of a Christian Bible*. The Bible in Ancient Christianity 13. Leiden: Brill, 2019.
Calderini, Aristide. *Dizionario dei nomi geografici e topografici dell'Egitto greco-romano*. Vol. 1. Cairo: Societá reale di geografia d'Egitto, 1935.
Collins, John J. "The Court-Tales in Daniel and the Development of Apocalyptic." *JBL* 94.2 (1975) 218–34.
———. *Daniel: A Commentary on the Book of Daniel*. Hermeneia. Minneapolis: Fortress, 1993.
———. *Daniel with an Introduction to Apocalyptic Literature*. FOTL 20. Grand Rapids: Eerdmans, 1984.
Crossan, John D. *The Cross That Spoke: The Origins of the Passion Narrative*. San Francisco: Harper & Row, 1988.
Davidova, S. "The Byzantine Synaxarion and Its Destiny in Russia." *Works of the Department of Old Russian Literature* 51 (1999) 58–79 (in Russian).
Dawes, Elizabeth, and Norman H. Baynes. *Three Byzantine Saints: Contemporary Biographies*. Oxford: Mowbrays, 1948.
Delehaye, Hippolyte. "Le Synaxaire de Sirmond." *AnBoll* 14 (1895) 396–434.
DiTommaso, Lorenzo. *The Book of Daniel and the Apocryphal Daniel Literature*. SVTP 20. Leiden: Brill, 2005.
Dulaey, Martine. "Les trois Hébreux dans la fournaise (Dn 3) dans l'interprétation symbolique de l'Église ancienne." *RevScRel* 71.1 (1997) 33–59.
Esbroeck, Michael van. "Three Hebrews in the Furnace." In *The Coptic Encyclopedia*, edited by Aziz Suryal Atiya, 7:2257–59. 8 vols. New York: Macmillan, 1991.
Evseev, Ivan. *The Book of Daniel in Old Slavonic Translation: Introduction and Texts*. Moscow: Lissner & Sovko, 1905.
Franko, Ivan. *Carpatho-Russian Literature of the XVII–XVIII Centuries*. Lviv: Shevchenko, 1900 (in Ukrainian).
———. *Collected Works in 50 volumes*. Vol. 30. Kyiv: Naukova Dumka, 1981 (in Ukrainian).
Galadza, Daniel. "Reading the Lives of the Saints in the Byzantine Rite: A Note on the Liturgical Context of the Martyrdom of Polycarp." Unpublished paper presented at the "Problems in the Early History of Liturgy" Seminar, North American Academy of Liturgy 2016 Annual Meeting, Houston, TX, 2016.

Bibliography

Gianelli, Cyrus, ed. *Codices Vaticani Graeci: Codices 1485–1683*. Vol. 5 of *Bibliothecae Apostolicae Vaticanae: Codices manu scripti recensiti*. Vatican: Typis Polyglottis Vaticanis, 1950.

Grillo, Jennie. *Daniel After Babylon: The Additions in the History of Interpretation. Reception of Old Testament Apocrypha*. Oxford: Oxford University Press, 2024.

Halkin, François. "La Passion ancienne des Saints Julien et Basilisse (BHG 970–971)." *AnBoll* 98.3–4 (1980) 241–96.

Humphreys, W. Lee. "A Life-Style for Diaspora: A Study of the Tales of Esther and Daniel." *JBL* 92 (1973) 211–23.

Johnson, Maxwell E. "The Apostolic Tradition." In *The Oxford History of Christian Worship*, edited by Geoffrey Wainwright and Karen B. Westerfield Tucker, 32–75. Oxford: Oxford University Press, 2006.

Jong, Albert de. *Traditions of the Magi: Zoroastrianism in Greek and Latin Literature*. RGRW 133. Leiden: Brill, 1977.

Joslyn-Siemiatkoski, Daniel. *Christian Memories of the Maccabean Martyrs*. New York: Palgrave Macmillan, 2009.

Kellermann, Ulrich. "Das Danielbuch und die Märtyrertheologie der Auferstehung." In *Die Entstehung der Jüdischen Martyrologie*, edited by Jan Willem van Henten, 51–70. StPB. Leiden: Brill, 1989.

Kraemer, Casper J., ed. *Excavations at Nessana (Auja Hafir)*. Vol. 3: *Non-Literary Papyri*. Princeton: Princeton University Press, 1958.

Lampe, G. W. H., ed. *Greek Patristic Lexicon*. Oxford: Clarendon, 1961.

Latte, Kurt, and Ian C. Cunningham, eds. *Hesychii Alexandrini Lexicon*. Vol. 2a. SGLG 11/2a. Berlin: de Gruyter, 2020.

Lund, Jerome Alan. *The Book of the Laws of the Countries. A Dialogue on Free Will Versus Fate: A Key-Word-in-Context Concordance*. Piscataway, NJ: Gorgias, 2007.

McLay, Tim. *The OG and Th Versions of Daniel*. Septuagint and Cognate Studies Series 43. Atlanta: Scholars, 1996.

Mécérian, Jean. "Introduction à l'étude des Synaxaires Arméniens." *Bulletin Arménologique (Mélange de l'Université Saint-Joseph)* 30 (1953) 99–188.

Meimaris, Yiannis E. *Sacred Names, Saints, Martyrs and Church Officials in the Greek Inscriptions and Papyri Pertaining to the Christian Church in Palestine*. ΜΕΛΕΤΗΜΑΤΑ 2. Athens: National Hellenic Research Foundation, 1986.

Merras, Merja. *The Origins of the Celebration of the Christian Feast of Epiphany: An Ideological, Cultural and Historical Study*. Joensuu, Finland: Joensuu University Press, 1995.

Milkov, Vladimir. "Directory of Ancient Russian Apocryphal Texts Representing the Concepts of Earthly Paradise." *Language and Text* 5.4 (2018) 49–67 (in Russian).

Murray, Robert. "The Origin of Aramaic ʿîr, Angel." *Or* 53 (1984) 303–17.

Nersessian, Vrej. "Eastern Christian Hagiographical Traditions: Oriental Orthodox: Armenian Hagiography." In *The Blackwell Companion to Eastern Christianity*, edited by Ken Parry, 458–61. Blackwell Companions to Religion. Oxford: Blackwell, 2007.

Nickelsburg, George W. E. *Resurrection, Immortality, and Eternal Life in Intertestamental Judaism and Early Christianity*. Expanded ed. Cambridge: Harvard University Press, 2006.

Nikitin, S., A. Tkachenko, and A. Lukashevich. "The Children in Babylon." In *OE* 6:481–86 (in Russian).

Bibliography

Olariu, Daniel. *Theodotion's Greek Text of Daniel: An Analysis of the Revisional Process and Its Semitic Source.* Supplements to the Textual History of the Bible 7. Leiden: Brill, 2023.

Osburn, Carrol D. "Methodology in Identifying Patristic Citations in NT Textual Criticism." *NovT* 47 (2005) 313–43.

Quarles, Charles. "ΜΕΤΑ ΤΗΝ ΕΓΕΡΣΙΝ ΑΥΤΟΥ A Scribal Interpolation in Matthew 27:53?" *TC: A Journal of Biblical Textual Criticism* 20 (2015) 1–15.

Rassart-Debergh, Marguerite. "Biblical Subjects in Coptic Art: The Three Hebrews in the Furnace." In *The Coptic Encyclopedia,* edited by Aziz Suryal Atiya, 2:388–90. 8 vols. New York: Macmillan, 1991.

Ross, William A. "Introduction." In *T&T Clark Handbook of Septuagint Research,* edited by William A. Ross and W. Edward Glenny, 1–5. London: T. & T. Clark, 2021.

Ruether, Rosemary Radford. "The Adversus Judaeos Tradition in the Church Fathers: The Exegesis of Christian Anti-Judaism." In *Aspects of Jewish Culture in the Middle Ages,* edited by Paul E. Szarmach, 27–50. Albany: SUNY Press, 1979.

Sarrazin, Roxanne Bélanger. "'Just as You Quenched the Fiery Furnace of Nebuchadnezzar, Also Quench Every Fever.' The Three Holy Children in Coptic Magic." *VC* 78 (2024) 58–86.

Screnock, John. "The Septuagint and Textual Criticism of the Hebrew Bible." In *T&T Clark Handbook of Septuagint Research,* edited by William A. Ross and W. Edward Glenny, 135–47. London: T. & T. Clark, 2021.

Seeliger, Hans Reinhard. "Παλαι Μαρτυρες. Die drei Jünglinge im Feuerofen als Typos in der spätantiken Kunst, Liturgie und patristischen Literatur: mit einigen Hinweisen zur Hermeneutik der christlichen Archäologie." In *Liturgie und Dichtung: Ein interdisziplinäres Kompendium II,* edited by H. Becker and R. Kaczynski, 257–334. Pietas Liturgica 2. Emming: St. Ottilien, 1983.

Somov, Alexey B. "The Martyrdom of Daniel and the Three Youths." *JSP* 30.4 (2021) 198–227.

———. *Representations of the Afterlife in Luke-Acts.* LNTS 556. London: T. & T. Clark, 2017.

Syroyid, Dariya. "Ancient Kyivan Tales in the Zamoysky Manuscript of the Early 16th Century." In *Studia o kulturze cerkiewnej w dawnej Rzeczypospolitej,* edited by Agnieszka Gronek and Alicja Z. Nowak, 27–42. Krakow: Scriptum, 2016 (in Ukrainian).

Theodoridis, Christos, ed. *Photii Patriarchae Lexicon.* Vol. 2. Berlin: de Gruyter, 1998.

Thomson, J. A. *Book of Jeremiah.* New International Commentary on the Old Testament. Grand Rapids: Eerdmans, 1980.

Tov, Emanuel. *Textual Criticism of the Hebrew Bible.* 2nd rev. ed. Minneapolis: Fortress, 2001.

Tucker, Dennis. "The Early Wirkungsgeschichte of Daniel 3: Representative Examples." *Journal of Theological Interpretation* 6 (2012) 295–306.

Turdeanu, Émil. "La légende du prophète Jérémie en roumain." In *Apocryphes Slaves et Roumains de L'Ancien Testament,* 306–47. SVTP 5. Leiden: Brill, 1981.

Vinson, Martha. "Gregory Nazianzen's Homily 15 and the Genesis of the Christian Cult of the Maccabean Martyrs." *Byzantion* 64 (1994) 166–92.

Wace, Henry, and William C. Piercy, eds. *A Dictionary of Christian Biography and Literature to the End of the Sixth Century A.D.* Boston: Little, Brown, 1911.

BIBLIOGRAPHY

Williams, A. Lukyn. *Adversus Judaeos: A Bird's-Eye View of the Christian Apologiae Until the Renaissance.* Cambridge: Cambridge University Press, 1935.

Wright, G. Ernest. "The Lawsuit of God." In *Israel's Prophetic Heritage: Essays in Honor of James Muilenberg*, edited by Bernhard W. Anderson and Walter Harrelson, 26–67. New York: Harper & Brothers, 1962.

Wright, N. T. *The Resurrection of the Son of God.* Christian Origins and the Question of God 3. Minneapolis: Fortress, 2003.

Ziadé, Raphaëlle. *Les martyrs Maccabées: De l'histoire juive au culte chrétien: les homélies de Grégoire de Nazianze et de Jean Chrysostome.* Supplements to Vigiliae Christianae 80. Leiden: Brill, 2007.

Index of Ancient Sources

Hebrew Bible/Old Testament

Genesis

2:8–10	31
3:24	26, 66
9:13	63
10:19	52
20–21	42
26:1	42
26:8–11	42
26:16	42
26:26	42
37–45	23

Exodus

3:2–14	30, 47, 61
3:2–5	62

Deuteronomy

2:23	52
11:29	52
22:12	67
27:2–4	52
27:13	52

Joshua

6:16	43, 58, 77
8:30	52
8:32–35	52
10:10	69
10:41	52
11:22	52
12:22	49
16:3	69
16:5	69

Judges

1:27	49
5:23	63
8:31	42
9:1–6	42
9:16–56	42
10:1	42

2 Samuel

11:21	42

2 Kings/4 Kingdoms

18:1–8	51
18:1–2	72, 82
18:13–37	76
18:13–16	41, 57
20:1–11	9, 51
20:3	51, 69, 64, 72, 80
20:6	51, 69, 64, 72, 80
20:18	57
21:1	9, 50
23:29	42
23:30	42
24–25	24

Index of Ancient Sources

2 Kings/4 Kingdoms (continued)

24:10—25:17	43, 59, 77
25:1	41, 57, 76
25:10	43, 58
25:11–17	84
25:11	44, 59, 77

1 Chronicles

18:16	42

2 Chronicles

29–31	51
32:24–26	51
32:27–30	51
35:22	49
36:17–20	43, 59, 77, 83

Esther

	23
8:12	80
9:24	80

Psalms

	6
19:3 LXX	63
31:4 LXX	44, 59, 77
31:9 LXX	59
34:1	42
54:11 LXX	41
73:7 LXX	83
78:1–3 LXX	83
82:8 LXX	52
88:20 LXX	63
88:31 LXX	40, 57, 75
131:8 LXX	27, 40, 76
136 LXX	25, 27
136:1–4 LXX	45, 60, 78
136:5–6 LXX	83
136:7 LXX	83
136:8 LXX	83
136:9 LXX	83
137:1 LXX	83
143:12–13 LXX	64
143:15 LXX	64

Isaiah

	6, 26
1:16–17	27, 40, 57, 76
1:21	27, 40, 57, 76
1:22–23	27, 40, 76
7:14	27, 40, 47, 62, 76, 79
8:8	47, 62, 79
9:5	29
16:17	57
36:1–22	76
36:1	41, 57
38	51
38:3	51, 64, 69, 72, 80
38:5	51, 64, 69, 72, 80
39:7	57, 82
51:3	31
52–53	23

Jeremiah

29:6 LXX	42, 58, 76
36:4	42
38:6–13	42
39:16–18	42
45:2–5	42
45:7 LXX	42
47:1	42
47:6	42, 58
52:12–23	77
52:12–14	83
52:13–23	43, 59
52:13	58
52:14	43, 58
52:15	44, 59, 77

Lamentations

5:15	41

Ezekiel

1:1	45

27:9	53	6:22	62
28:13	31	7–12	2
31:8	31	7–8	72
36:33–35	31	7	7, 27
		7:7–8	73
		8–12	2
		11	72
		11:33	73
		11:35–38	2
		12:2–3	2–3, 54
		12:11–12	2
		12:13	1, 54, 71

Daniel

	1–3, 13, 27
1–6	2, 5, 22, 62
1–4	25
1–3	27
1	1–2
1:1–7	72
1:1	41, 57, 69, 76
1:2	43, 59, 77
1:3–6	69, 82
1:3	50
1:6	51, 71
1:7	70, 82
1:12	72
2–6	2
2	7, 46, 60, 72, 77
2:27	61
2:46	70
2:48	70, 72
2:49	1
3	1–4, 6–8, 14, 23, 34–35, 40, 47
3:1–23	70, 72, 78, 85
3:1	46, 60, 78, 84
3:8–23	46, 61
3:21	36
3:26	85
3:27–28	70
3:27	47, 78, 85
3:28–29	85
3:28	72
3:30	1, 71
3:92	61
4	26, 72
4:9	70
4:10–14	62
4:13	85
4:29–37	85
4:31–34	63
5:29	14, 73
6	1–3, 7, 23, 34, 73

Theodotion Daniel

3:1–88	3
3:1	84
3:13–23	29
3:24	85
3:47–50	85
3:47	61
3:49–51	47, 61, 70, 72, 78
3:49	29
3:51–90	3
3:88	3
3:91–92	29, 47, 70
3:92	26, 51, 61–62, 78
3:93–97	79
3:93–94	48
3:94	61, 78
3:95–97	48, 63
4:13–17	8
4:13	26, 47, 62, 79
9:24	47

OG Daniel

3:92	47
4:13	62

Amos

	6
5:27	27, 40–41, 43, 57, 76
8:10	27, 40–41, 43, 57–58, 76–77

Index of Ancient Sources

Micah
27, 40–41

Habakkuk
1:6–10	41, 57, 76

Deuterocanonical Works

Tobit
23

Judith
1:1	32
8:17	63

Wisdom of Solomon
1–6	23
3:7	51, 66

1 Baruch
1:4	45

Epistle of Jeremiah
3–5	46, 60
4–5	78

Song of the Three Youths
	3
66	3

Susanna
23

Bel and the Dragon
	48, 86
3	46, 60, 78
1–27	7

23–27	46, 60
23	78
28–42	7, 73
36	62

1 Maccabees
1:56	39
2:59	4
6:2	80
9:22	39
10:15	39
12:15	63
16:23	39

2 Maccabees
6–7	3
7	2–4, 23, 33
7:9	4
7:14	4
7:23	4
12:11	63
14:18	39

3 Maccabees
23

4 Maccabees
	3–4, 23, 33
1:8	39
16:3	3
16:21	3

Pseudepigrapha

2 Baruch
21:1	42

4 Baruch
	7, 25, 42
3:10	42
3:12–13	42

Index of Ancient Sources

3:14	42
3:15–16	43, 58, 77
3:15	42
3:21–22	42
4	42
4:7–12	42, 58
4:10–11	25
5:1–2	43, 58, 77
5:2	42
5:25	42
6:2	42

1 Enoch

1–36	62
1:5	62
10:7	62
12:3	62
32:3–4	31
62–63	23
77:3	31

2 Enoch

8:1–10	31

Greek Apocalypse of Ezra

1:12	31
5:20–22	31

Life of Adam and Eve

40	52

Lives of the Prophets

	5, 15
4:1–2	25
4:1	69
4:2	69
4:21	1

Testament of Levi

6:1	53

Testament of Moses

9	23

Vision of Ezra

58–59	31
64	31

Dead Sea Scrolls

4QApocryphon of Daniel ar [4Q246]	5
Prayer of Nabonidus [4Q242]	5
4QPseudo-Daniel^a [4Q243]	5
4QPseudo-Daniel^b [4Q244]	5
4QPseudo-Daniel^c [4Q245]	5

Josephus

Jewish Antiquities

	5

Rabbinical Works

Babylonian Talmud

Sanhedrin

93a	70

Genesis Rabbah

96.5	70

Pirqe Rabbi Eliezer

33	4

Shir Ha-Shirim Rabbah

7.8	70

Targum Pseudo-Jonathan

Deuteronomy

34.6	52

Classical and Greco-Roman Literature

Herodotus

Histories

2.159	42

Pseudo-Callisthenes

Alexandria

	16

New Testament

Matthew

1:25	28, 47, 61
2	49
2:1	28, 47, 49, 61
27:45–53	30
27:51–53	10, 54, 65, 81
27:51	30,
27:52–53	5, 26, 28, 31, 87
27:53	55

Mark

13:32–37	41
15:33	65

Luke

2:4–7	28, 47, 61
2:25–35	31
21:34–36	41
23:40–43	10, 26, 66
23:43	28, 66

John

12:28–29	63
13:27	51

1 Corinthians

15:6	10, 26, 28, 30, 54, 66, 81
15:22–23	30
15:24	73

Galatians

4:9	39, 56, 61, 75

1 Thessalonians

2:14–15	34
5:3–7	41

Hebrews

	26
11:34	4

Jude

1:9	52

Revelation

10:1	63
16:16	49
20:4	73
22:1	31
22:5	31

Early Christian Writings and Apocrypha

Acts of Andrew and Philemon

7:14–26	52

Index of Ancient Sources

Acts of Paul
14:5 — 67

Acta SS. Fructuosi, Augurii et Eulogii
4.2 — 29

Acts of Thecla
— 74

Apocalypse of Peter
16 — 31

Apocalypse of Pseudo-Ephrem
— 73

Apostolic Constitutions
5.1.5 — 14

Augustine

Tractatus adv. Judaeos
7.10 — 34

Sermons
286 — 3

Bardaisan of Edessa

Book of the Laws of the Countries
— 50

Barnabas
5.11 — 34

Basil the Great

Epistolae
258.4 — 49–50

Clement of Alexandria

Paedagogus
2.8.75.1–2 — 62

Stromateis
1.21.146.1–2 — 20
6.6.47–48 — 31

Cyprian

Epistles
6.3 — 4
58.5 — 4

Ad fortunatum
11 — 2

De lapsis
31 — 2

Ephrem the Syrian

Hymns on the Fast
app. 2.10 — 29

Hymns on the Nativity
8.6 — 29

Epiphanius of Salamis

Ancoratus
113.2.3 — 49

Life of the Prophet Daniel and About His Tomb
PG 43:404–5 — 19

Index of Ancient Sources

Panarion

3.512.18	49
3.512.23	49

Epistle of Pseudo-Dionysius the Areopagite to Timothy

9:11–19	52

Eusebius of Caesarea

Demenstratio evangelica

1.1.7	34

Eclogae propheticae

3.43	29

Praeparatio evangelica

6.10.16.4	49
6.10.38.3	49

Gospel of Nicodemus

	31
9–10	26
10	66
17:3	31

Gregory of Nazianzus

Homilies

5.40	2

Gregory of Nyssa

In diem natalem

PG 46:1136B	62

Hippolytus

Commentarium in Danielum

2.28.3–5	4
2.29.12	4
2.30.1	1
2.32.6–2.34.3	29
2.33.4	29
2.35.8–9	1
3.7.40	63
3.9.1	62
3.9.6	62
3.16	70
4.5.1–3	73
4.9.2–3	73

Ignatius of Antioch

To the Magnesians

9.2	31

Irenaeus of Lyons

Adversus haereses

3.6.2	62
4.10.1	62
4.20.11	29
5.5.2	4, 29

Epideixis tou apostolikou kērygmatos

46	61–62

Isidor of Pelusium

Book 2 Letter 177 to Presbyter Theodotus

18–22	62
20	62

Index of Ancient Sources

Jeremiah Apocryphon

30	25, 44
31	45
33	25, 45

John Chrysostom

Adversus Judaeos

1.7.2	34
1.7.5	34
5.9.5	34

John of Damascus

Epistula ad Theophilum imperatorem de sacris imaginibus

11	49

Justin

Dialogus cum Tryphone

17.1	34
39.1	34
59.1	61
127.4	61

Lactantius

Divinarum institutionum

4.10.18	34
4.11.3	34

Leontius of Byzantium

Contra Nestorianos

3.1376.32	49
3.1384.40	49

Martyrdom of Daniel and the Three Youths

1:1–4	6
1:3	23
1:4	56
1:5–9	6
1:6	26, 28
1:7	27–28, 57
1:8	32
1:10–11	7, 32
1:11–13	7
1:11	76
1:12–13	25
1:13	76–77
1:14–17	7
1:14	36
2:1–4	7, 25
2:5–6	7, 25
2:7–8	7
2:9	7
3	10, 47
3:1–3	7
3:1	34
3:3	7, 21
3:4–5	8
3:4	29
3:6–9	29
3:6	8, 61
3:5	8, 29
3:7	8, 28–29, 51
3:8–10	8
3:8–9	26
3:10	29
3:13	31
4:1–2	8, 34
4:1	32
4:2	33
4:3–7	8
4:4–5	50
4:4	70
4:6	32
4:7	32–33
4:8–9	9

Index of Ancient Sources

Martyrdom of Daniel and the Three Youths (continued)

4:8	32
4:9–10	66
4:9	9, 28
5:1–3	9
5:1	36
5:4–5	34
5:4	9, 30, 33–34
5:5	9, 20, 30, 34
5:6–9	26, 30, 36, 65, 67
5:6	9, 18, 28, 34
5:7	9
5:8–9	10, 28
5:8	9, 31
5:9	82
5:10	9–10, 20, 71

Martyrdom of Julian and Basilissa

13.16	62

Martyrdom of Perpetua and Felicity

4.22	31
4.26	31
11.11	31
11.15	31

Martyrdom of Polycarp

14.2	31

Martyrdom of Tarachus, Probus and Andronicus

7	14

Martyrdom of Theodotus

1.12	14

Nessana Papyri

90.170	19
90.185	19

Origen

Commentarius in Canticum

2.8.8	62

Commentarii in Romanos

10.8.5	62

Panegyric of the Three Children of Babylon

	14
70	50
86–88	54
89	54
91–92	44
97	54
99	54
110	54

Polychronius of Apamea

Commentarii in Danielem

4.23.2	62

Pseudo-Bachios of Maiuma

On the Three Children

	46

Pseudo-Clement

Recognitions

20.20–21	49

Pseudo-Cyprian

De laude martyrii

12	4

De pascha computes

17	4

Pseudo-Cyril of Alexandria

Miracles of the Three Youths

	19

Pseudo-John Chrysostom

De tribus pueris et de fornace Babylonica

PG 56:593–600	2
PG 56:600	70

Sermo de obitu sanctorum trium puerorum

1:1–4	11, 6
1:1	60–61
1:3	23, 29
1:4	36
1:5–9	6
1:6	26
1:7	27
1:8	32
1:10–11	7, 32
1:12–13	25
1:13	81
1:14–17	7
2:1–4	7, 25
2:5–6	7, 25
2:7–8	7
2:9	7
3	30
3:1–3	7
3:1	34, 63
3:4–5	8
3:4	7, 29
3:5	8
3:6–9	29
3:6	8
3:7	8, 28–30
3:8–10	8
3:8–9	26, 36
3:13	31
4:1–2	8, 34
4:1	32
4:2	33
4:3–7	8
4:4	70
4:5	32
4:8–10	9
4:8	32
4:9	51
4:10	9, 28, 34
4:11–15	11, 26, 30, 36
4:11	10, 28
4:12	10
4:13–15	10, 28
4:13	31, 55
4:14	10, 26, 28, 66
4:15	65
4:16–17	9
4:16	36
5:1–3	9
5:1	36
5:4–5	34
5:4	9, 30, 33
5:5–7	10
5:5	9, 20, 30, 34
5:6–8	11
5:6	21–22
5:8	9, 52

Tertullian

Adversus Marcionem

4.10.12	29
4.21.8	29

Adversus Praxean

16.6	29, 62

Index of Ancient Sources

De anima

55.4	31

De resurrectione carnis

58.6–10	4

Theodoret of Cyrus

Interpretatio in Danielem

PG 81:1360	62

Theodosius of Alexandria

On the Archangel Michael

	46

Theophilus of Alexandria

Sermon on the Three Youths of Babylon

	19

Later Christian Writings

Alexandria, 2nd ed.

	74
2.17	16, 37, 53

Alexandria, 3rd ed.

	16

Alexandria, 4th ed.

	74
2.17	16, 37, 53

Armenian Synaxarion, 2nd ed.

	15, 53, 55

Armenian Synaxarion, 4th ed.

	15, 19, 32, 53

Constantinus Manasses

Synopsis Chronike

5197	57
6355	57

Dmitry of Rostov

Life of Daniel and the Three Youths

	14, 32

Georgius Hamartolus

Chronicon breve

110:141	50

Great Menaion Reader

	11, 14, 17, 36, 40–41, 44–45, 50, 52–53, 76–77
fol. 302r	14
fols. 304r–305v	11
fols. 305v–307v	11
fols. 331r–336v	11
fol. 335r	67
fols. 337r–337v	14

Krekhiv Palaea

fols. 953–955	12

Jacobite Arabic Synaxarium (*Syn. Alex.*)

	18
PO 16:247	50
PO 16:353–54	53

Index of Ancient Sources

Menologion of Basil II

13–15, 35, 48, 72–73

PG 117:19–614 — 13
PG 117:212 — 17, 37
Vat. gr. 1613
fols. 251r–252v — 13, 35

Prolog

12, 14, 72

Serbian Alexandria

16

Sophronius of Jerusalem

Vita Cyri et Joannis

3–5 — 19

Stephen Teslevtsiv Manuscript (UkS)

7, 11–12, 36–37, 48, 55–56

1:1 — 77, 87
1:8 — 59
2:7 — 29
3:12 — 52
3:13 — 31, 77
3:14 — 20, 71

Synaxarion of Constantinople

11–12, 14–15, 18, 25

317–320 — 13, 17, 37
317 — 25
319 — 13, 20, 30, 52–53, 55
320 — 20

The Tale of the Captivity of Jerusalem

25

Vita Sancti Danielis stylitae

19

Vita sancti Macarii Romani

Vassiliev 137 — 53

Yerevan, Matenadaran, 1500 Manuscript (Arm.)

fol. 362r — 15, 32, 53

Zamość Manuscript (SlavZ)

12, 36–37, 40–41, 43–49, 51–55, 80

1:13 — 81
4:6 — 33, 50
5:5 — 53
5:10 — 71

www.ingramcontent.com/pod-product-compliance
Lightning Source LLC
Chambersburg PA
CBHW031349160426
43196CB00007B/796